Step In!

Salesian Bible Meditations
Volume 2: Christology

Meditations Written by Tom Vresics
Meditative Artwork by Amy Vresics

Dedicated to my loving wife Jan,
my amazing daughters Erin and Amy
and my supportive Salesian family
throughout the world.

Live Jesus!

Volume 2: Christology in Light of the Trinity

The illustrations or icons in our first volume of *Step In!*
Salesian Bible Meditations: Revelation, were added to help introduce
the practice of Lectio Divina and, of course, the practice of Iconic
Lectio. In that volume we focused primarily upon the stories of the Old
Testament along with related teachings from Saint Francis de Sales.
Judging from the positive response we received from both teachers and
students alike, we decided to publish a second book.

In this volume of *Step In!* *Salesian Bible Meditations:*
Christology, our focus is to highlight Jesus' Christological identity in
relationship to the other members of the Trinity. This is simply a fancy
theological phrase meaning Jesus' identity as both fully human and
fully divine. Throughout this volume we seek to show Jesus acting in
relationship to both the Father and the Holy Spirit rather than alone.
The purpose for this is to help everyone understand that God prefers us
to act within our community of faith, the Church. Just as each member
of the Trinity glorifies and is glorified in the presence and activity of
the other members of the Trinity, so we should rejoice to be part of and
act with other members of the Church.

Another feature found in this volume is plenty of pictures with
angels holding scrolls with prophecies from the prophet Isaiah. The
angels are there simply as messengers of God the Father, as the word
"angel" implies. Other times the Father will be represented as a hand
from Heaven or as a beam of light streaming from the heavens.
Isaiah's prophecies are featured in this volume due to their Messianic
and Christological importance plus the fact that Jeremiah's prophecy
was used to represent the prophetic tradition in volume one. The Holy
Spirit, in turn, will be represented as a dove with a halo or as swirls of
wind as the "ru'ah elohim" or "breath of God" or by tongues of fire.

If you like this volume and have not read *Step In! Salesian*
Bible Meditations: Revelation, we strongly suggest that you get a
copy. We also want you to know that we will continue to publish
further volumes in this series to complement the High School Religion
Curriculum Framework produced by the United States Catholic
Bishops. The next volume will highlight stories from both the Old and
New Testaments along with the themes of the original goodness of
creation, individual and social sin and God's redemptive and saving
work in both Salvation History and in our personal lives through grace.

Table of Contents

Lectio Divina #1 The Christ Child   Pages 4-9

LectioDivina #2 Jesus Our Brother   Pages 10-15

Lectio Divina #3 Christ Who Calls Us   Pages 16-21

Lectio Divina #4 Christ the Teacher   Pages 22-27

Lectio Divino #5 Christ the Healer   Pages 28-33

Lectio Divina #6 Christ the Storyteller   Pages 34-39

Lectio Divina #7 Christ the Humble Servant   Pages 40-45

Lectio Divina #8 Christ the Suffering Servant Pages 46-51

Lectio Divina #9 Christ Our Redeemer   Pages 52-57

Lectio Divina #10 The Risen Christ   Pages 58-63

Lectio Divina #11 Christ Who Sends the Spirit   Pages 64-69

Lectio Divina #12 Christ in Scripture and Tradition Pages 70-75

Lectio Divina #13 Jesus and Life in the Spirit   Pages 76-81

Lectio Divina #14 Christ the Alpha and Omega   Pages 82-87

Christological Color Images for Iconic Lectio   Pages 88-95

Appendix: Pages 96-112
- The Introduction to the Devout Life   Page 96
- The Decision to Live the Devout Life   Page 98
- Prayer and Sacraments   Page 100
- Choice and Exercise of the Virtues   Page 102
- Temptation   Page 104
- Self-Renewal   Page 106
- Application for Today and Jesus Icon Reflections Page 108
- Bibliography/Acknowledgements/Notes   Page 110

The Christ Child

Luke 2:1,3-7

Also Emmanuel (Matthew 1:23) and Son of David (Mark 10:46-52)

Background

What is the most thoughtful loving gift that anyone has ever given you? Most likely the person giving you that gift knew what you wanted more than anything else. He/she probably also had to put a lot of his/her own time and effort to make the gift extra special.

Think of all the effort and time the Trinity put into the gift of the Incarnation. God the Father graced Mary with the Immaculate Conception, freeing her from original sin so she could truly be the Mother of God's Son. Recall the rest of the Father's plan of salvation from Abraham, Moses, and David to Joseph who adopted Jesus.

Consider that the Holy Spirit conceived Jesus in Mary's womb in response to Mary's "yes" leading to Jesus' Virgin birth. Also recall that the Holy Spirit inspired the prophets and the writers of the Bible to prepare the Chosen People for the Messiah's birth.

Finally, think of the Son of God, who though equal to God, emptied himself to become human like us in all things but sin. When the Son of God assumed our human nature, he also accepted suffering and death, but more importantly he also became the gift of God's love made real by being born into the human family.

Each Christmas take time to reflect on how great a gift we all have received in Jesus who is truly "Emmanuel" or "God with us."

Salesian Concept
Salesian Optimism
Part II

In a Christmas Eve sermon in 1620, Saint Francis de Sales preached, **"It is not the Father alone who brings about the Incarnation, but also the Son and the Holy Spirit. And, even though the Holy Spirit has taken part in this mystery; nevertheless it is only the second Person who became Incarnate..."** De Sales continues by saying that the hypostatic union of Jesus' human and divine natures still exists. [1]

If Jesus' human nature still co-exists with his divine nature in heaven, then our humanity is really something special. This should help us see not only the goodness of our humanity, but also the goodness of our human relationships. This means we will continue to share in the same loving relationships in heaven that we now experience in life.

Imagine your joy when you see your loved ones in heaven who have died before you in faith, like your grandparents, great-grandparents, and others. Truly, this is another amazing gift of God to our humanity.

MEDITATION: A SALESIAN METHOD

1. Shift Gears from School Work to Prayer

a. Throw off all your concerns from the school day. *(Relax)*

b. Read Luke 2:1, 3-7 as well as Matthew 1:22-23 below.

In those days a decree went out from Caesar Augustus that the whole world should be enrolled. This was the first census, when Quirinius was governor of Syria. So all went to be enrolled, each to his own town. And Joseph too went up from Galilee from the town of Nazareth to Judea, to the city of David that is called Bethlehem, because he was of the house and family of David, to be enrolled with Mary, his betrothed, who was with child. While they were there, the time came for her to have her child, and she gave birth to her firstborn son. She wrapped him in swaddling clothes and laid him in a manger, because there was no room for them in the inn.

Matthew 1:22-23

All this took place to fulfill what the Lord had said through the prophet: "Behold, the virgin shall be with child and bear a son, and they shall name him Emmanuel," which means "God is with us."

2. Experience Face Time with God

a. Ask for a deeper awareness of God's presence

b. Ask for God's inspiration to pray sincerely.

3. Visualize the Story *(Ponder the story's sights, sounds, tastes, smells and feelings.)*

Imagine that you are in Bethlehem at the birth of Christ. You see two travelers among all the other people coming to Bethlehem for the census of Caesar Augustus. You notice that the woman is as pregnant as one can be before birth. As you see them turned away from the inn, what expressions of disappointment fill their faces? What expressions of gratitude and trust replace their disappointment as they are shown the way to the stable?

Think of how the stable looked with all the freshly stored hay made ready for bedding and feeding the animals. What preparations does Joseph make when he arrives for the comfort of Mary and for the soon to be born child Jesus? As Joseph sees the manger used for feeding animals, what thoughts fill his mind at the irony that a feeding trough will become a crib for the Son of God?

Now, listen to Mary as she is overcome with the pains of childbirth. Notice how expressions of joy quickly replace any trace of discomfort once Jesus is born. What are the words of praise coming from Mary's heart to God? What does she say to Joseph?

Watch as Joseph places Jesus in Mary's arms for the first time. What does Mary say to her child? How are both Mary and Joseph responding to the notion that this little bundle of joy is their child and the Son of God at the same time?

All of a sudden Mary and Joseph see you and motion for you to come. They give you the infant Jesus to hold. What sounds does Jesus make in your arms? What does his facial expression say to you?

4. Express Your Heart *(Write a three sentence spontaneous, heartfelt prayer.)*

What are you feeling as you see Mary and Joseph with Jesus? What type of praise and adoration can you place as your gift to the babe of Bethlehem? What is your heartfelt prayer to God for the gift of Jesus?

5. Be the Change *(Write a resolution that describes what you will do and when.)*

What do you feel you should do in order to live this day well in light of your meditation? Write one concrete resolution that can serve as your gift to Jesus, as Emmanuel or "God with us."

6. Text a Phrase *(Sum up your meditation into a text of around a 100 characters.)*

State within the confines of this spiritual journal the most helpful insight from your meditation. It can come from the Background, the Salesian Concept or your Salesian Meditation.

7. Create Word Art *(Express your text with visual art, poetry, music, or drama.)*

Express your Text a Phrase in a creative way that will help you recall your meditation with God throughout this day. Your art should help you respond sincerely to God's gift of Jesus.

See the color icon for the Christ Child on page 89.

Visualize the Story *(Write down your insights about God from this meditation.)*

_____

_____

_____

_____

_____

_____

_____

_____

_____

_____

_____

_____

_____

_____

_____

Express Your Heart *(Write a three sentence spontaneous, heartfelt prayer.)*

_____

_____

_____

_____

_____

_____

Be the Change *(Write a resolution that describes what you will do and when.)*

_____

_____

_____

Text a Phrase: *(Sum up your meditation into a text of around a 100 characters.)*

_____

_____

Create Word Art *(Express your text with visual art, poetry, music, or drama.)*

Jesus
Our Brother
Matthew 4:1-11

Also the Son of Man (Mark 14:62)
and Our Great High Priest
(Hebrews 2:17-18, 4:14-16, 10:26-28)

Background

Have you ever faced a challenge to test your readiness for a larger one? High school tests your readiness for college and college tests your readiness for work in the real world. Whatever your challenge, the temptation always exists to fail to live up to who you are.

After his baptism Jesus faced such a challenge. Jesus was sent out into the desert by the Holy Spirit to fast and pray before beginning his ministry. This is when the devil appeared to challenge Jesus' identity as the Son of God and throw him off track. While Jesus was the Son of God, he was also fully human, as the Son of Man. In Daniel 7:12-15 and Mark 14:62, the Son of Man is seen as the person who brings God's salvation in human history. Jesus' victory over the devil in the desert foreshadowed his defeat of sin and death on the cross. It also reversed the failure of our first parents to stand up to the deceit of the devil.

Hebrews 2:17-18 states that Jesus had to become like us in every way in order *"to be able to help those being tested."* Jesus' sacrificial obedience to God's will in his life and especially in his death makes him our Great High Priest. In Jesus, we have someone who can both sympathize with our suffering and serve as an example for all. Living up to our Baptismal promises, to turn away from sin and follow Jesus, is the truest way to live as brothers and sisters of Christ.

Salesian Concept

Facing Temptations

Even though he became a saint, Francis de Sales constantly faced temptations, like anger, throughout his life. To illustrate the importance of dealing with everyday temptations, De Sales dedicates the entire fourth part of the *Introduction to the Devout Life* to this topic.

When dealing with temptations De Sales makes four major points: 1) When tempted practice the opposite virtue. 2) Focus upon defeating smaller temptations, since they are more frequent and often lead us down the path to commit larger sins. 3) During temptations you should affectionately turn to Christ and share your most frequent temptations with your confessor. 4) Recognize that feeling a temptation is not the same as giving in to it, as long as any pleasure we feel is involuntary.

These habits **"will prevent you from looking at the temptation. And seeing that his efforts have no other result than to make your love of God increase, the devil will quickly cease bothering you."**[2]

MEDITATION: A SALESIAN METHOD

1.   Shift Gears from School Work to Prayer

      a. Throw off all your concerns from the school day. *(Relax)*

      b. Read Matthew 4:1-11 below.

Then Jesus was led by the Spirit into the desert to be tempted by the devil. He fasted for forty days and forty nights, and afterwards he was hungry. The tempter approached and said to him, "If you are the Son of God, command that these stones become loaves of bread." He said in reply, "It is written: 'One does not live by bread alone, but by every word that comes forth from the mouth of God.'"

Then the devil took him to the holy city, and made him stand on the parapet of the temple, and said to him, "If you are the Son of God, throw yourself down. For it is written: 'He will command his angels concerning you and with their hands they will support you, lest you dash your foot against a stone.'" Jesus answered him, "Again it is written, 'You shall not put the Lord, your God, to the test.'"

Then the devil took him up to a very high mountain, and showed him all the kingdoms of the world in their magnificence, and he said to him, "All these I shall give to you, if you will prostrate yourself and worship me." At this, Jesus said to him, "Get away, Satan! It is written: 'The Lord, your God, shall you worship and him alone shall you serve.'" Then the devil left him and, behold, angels came and ministered to him.

2. Experience Face Time with God

      a. Ask for a deeper awareness of God's presence.

      b. Ask for God's inspiration to pray sincerely.

3. Visualize the Story *(Ponder the story's sights, sounds, tastes, smells and feelings.)*

      Picture the desert beyond the Jordan River, heat, scrub brush, stones, and arid mountains. Think of your sense of isolation from others, just you, your thoughts and plans. Suddenly, you see Jesus. It is clear that he has already been out in the desert for days fasting and praying. You can see that he is determined to follow his Father's plan to bring forth the Reign of God and defeat the Reign of Sin and Evil. What does Jesus look like to you? What plans do you think Jesus is making?

      The Devil makes his first attack upon Jesus to urge him to prove that he is God by turning stones into bread. How does Jesus' response show that even though his hunger is a sign of his humanity, his love for God is his divine source of strength against any temptation?

Next, Jesus refuses to prove his divinity by jumping from the highest peak of the Temple. How does this relate to Jesus' practice of refusing to perform miracles for those without faith, such as Pilate?

Lastly, Jesus refuses to bow down and worship the devil to win the souls of all humanity. Does Jesus think the Devil's idea will actually work? What expression does the devil have when he realizes that Jesus is onto his subtle lies and tricks?

As the devil leaves Jesus, what emotion do you see etched upon Jesus' face: growing confidence, relief, determination, or something else? In what ways do you imagine the angels ministered to Jesus: bringing him food, giving him an encouraging message from the Father, or showing him a vision of heaven filled with all the souls, including yours, that his faithfulness to God's plan had won?

4. Express Your Heart *(Write a three sentence spontaneous, heartfelt prayer.)*

What do you feel as you see Jesus withstand temptation? What can you say to God for the times you failed to follow Jesus' example when you were being tempted? What words can you use to call to mind that Jesus is present with you in the midst of all your temptations?

5. Be the Change *(Write a resolution describing what you will do and when.)*

What do you feel you should do in order to live this day well in light of your meditation? Write one concrete resolution that can serve as your response to follow Jesus' example and Saint Francis de Sales' teachings about resisting temptation.

6. Text a Phrase *(Sum up your meditation into a text of around a 100 characters.)*

State within the confines of this spiritual journal the most helpful insight from your meditation. It can come from the Background, the Salesian Concept or your Salesian Meditation.

7. Create Word Art *(Express your text with visual art, poetry, music, or drama.)*

Express your Text a Phrase in a creative way that will help you recall your meditation with God throughout this day. Your art should help you look for the compassionate help of God in the midst of every temptation.

13

See the color icon for Jesus Our Brother on page 89.

Visualize the Story *(Write down your insights about God from this meditation.)*

_____

_____

_____

_____

_____

_____

_____

_____

_____

_____

_____

_____

_____

_____

_____

Express Your Heart *(Write a three sentence spontaneous, heartfelt prayer.)*

_____

_____

_____

_____

_____

_____

Be the Change *(Write a resolution that describes what you will do and when.)*

_____

_____

_____

Text a Phrase: *(Sum up your meditation into a text of around a 100 characters.)*

_____

_____

Create Word Art *(Express your text with visual art, poetry, music, or drama.)*

Christ
Who Calls Us
Mark 1:14b-22

Also the Messiah (Matthew 11:1-6)
and Son of God (Matthew 16: 13-20)

Background

Did you ever wish that you could take a year off from school or work to do something out of the ordinary? Imagine going away from your normal surroundings to do something unique, something that few people ever get the opportunity to do. If you were presented with this opportunity to put your normal life on hold, would you do it?

In the Jewish culture in which Jesus lived, young men were offered the opportunity to study the Torah with a learned rabbi for a year. This sabbatical year, a year of rest from normal work, was based upon the Jewish practice of the Sabbath rest. Just as taking one day to rest each week is necessary to renew us for our work and weekly activities, so a year away from one's regular occupation was seen as necessary in Jesus' culture to renew and strengthen individuals for their life's work. In Jesus' day, families would help support parents whose sons made this kind of Sabbatical. This was because their sons would later benefit the community with their better understanding of the Law of Moses.

In this Gospel Peter, Andrew, James and John are not being called by any ordinary rabbi or teacher of the Law, but by Jesus, the Eschatological (Final) Prophet, the Messiah and the Son of God. We too are called to journey with Christ who is *"gentle and humble of heart."* (Matthew 11:29)

Salesian Concept
The Universal Call to Holiness

We can often feel that it is only priests, sisters and brothers whom God uses in a special way to do his work. As Salesians we need to recall that we are also called to be holy or **"Live Jesus"** in the present moments of our lives. The Second Vatican Council (1962-1965) echoed the teachings of Saint Francis de Sales concerning the role of the laity in the Church, and the Universal Call to Holiness in *Lumen Gentium.*[3]

As you consider your role as a non-ordained member of the Church think of these words of Saint Francis: **"Each of us has been given a unique vocation in life, which only we can fulfill."**[4] There are people who may only come to friendship in Christ because of the unique gifts and personality only you can share. If Jesus could use ordinary fishermen to spread the Gospel, he can surely use any of us.

MEDITATION: A SALESIAN METHOD

1. Shift Gears from School Work to Prayer

    a. Throw off all your concerns from the school day. *(Relax)*

    b. Read Mark 1:14b-22 below.

Jesus came to Galilee proclaiming the gospel of God: "This is the time of fulfillment. The kingdom of God is at hand. Repent, and believe in the gospel." As he passed by the Sea of Galilee, he saw Simon and his brother Andrew casting their nets into the sea; they were fishermen. Jesus said to them, "Come after me, and I will make you fishers of men." Then they abandoned their nets and followed him. He walked along a little farther and saw James, the son of Zebedee, and his brother John. They too were in a boat mending their nets. Then he called them. So they left their father Zebedee in the boat along with the hired men and followed him. Then they came to Capernaum, and on the Sabbath he entered the synagogue and taught. The people were astonished at his teaching, for he taught them as one having authority and not as the scribes.

2. Experience Face Time with God

    a. Ask for a deeper awareness of God's presence.

    b. Ask for God's inspiration to pray sincerely.

3. Visualize the Story *(Ponder the story's sights, sounds, tastes, smells and feelings.)*

Picture the shore of the Sea of Galilee. Imagine the small whitewashed homes of the fishermen and their boats and nets lined up a short distance away. See Jesus as he watches the fishermen readying themselves to take their boats and nets out to fish. The day is sunny and warm. Fathers are shouting instructions to their sons to make sure everything is as it should be.

Notice Jesus as he comes across Peter and Andrew. Jesus approaches them and says: *"Come, follow me, and I will make you fishers of men."* What is their reaction to Jesus' invitation? How do their facial expressions reflect their heartfelt emotions?

What is special about the physical presence of Jesus in this scene? What kind of facial expression does Jesus have as they accept his offer to follow Him? As you see them leave their nets, what do you notice as you watch them walking off together? What are they saying?

Now, Jesus walks by James and John who are each working on a separate boat with men hired to be on their father's crew. Jesus calls James and John from all the other men. The two brothers pick other men to take their places before they join Jesus. What is their father's facial expression? What is he saying? What is your reaction?

What is it about Jesus that gets Peter, Andrew, James and John to leave their nets and follow him? Jesus now turns to you and says, "You too, come follow me."

4. Express Your Heart *(Write a three sentence spontaneous, heartfelt prayer.)*

What are you feeling as you watch Jesus and hear him speak with the first disciples walking on the shore? How is Jesus calling you to follow him as a disciple and a friend today? What heartfelt emotions do you have as Jesus invites you? Take time to ponder God's offer in your heart. What things might you have to leave behind to follow Jesus?

5. Be the Change *(Write a resolution that describes what you will do and when.)*

What do you feel you should do in order to live this day well in light of your meditation? Write one concrete, do-able resolution that can serve as your reply to Jesus' invitation to *"Come and follow me."*

6. Text a Phrase *(Sum up your meditation into a text of around a 100 characters.)*

State within the confines of this spiritual journal the most helpful insight from your meditation. It can come from the Background, the Salesian Concept or your Salesian Meditation.

7. Create Word Art *(Express your text with visual art, poetry, music, or drama.)*

Express your Text a Phrase in a creative way that will help you recall your meditation with God throughout this day. Your art should help you follow Jesus as a disciple and as a friend.

See the color icon for Christ Who Calls Us on page 90.

Visualize the Story *(Write down your insights about God from this meditation.)*

_____

_____

_____

_____

_____

_____

_____

_____

_____

_____

_____

_____

_____

_____

Express Your Heart *(Write a three sentence spontaneous, heartfelt prayer.)*

_____

_____

_____

_____

_____

_____

Be the Change *(Write a resolution that describes what you will do and when.)*

_____

_____

_____

Text a Phrase: *(Sum up your meditation into a text of around a 100 characters.)*

_____

_____

Create Word Art *(Express your text with visual art, poetry, music, or drama.)*

Christ the Teacher

Matthew 5:1-12

Also the Eschatological or Final Prophet (Matthew 12:41-42)

Background

Have you ever heard a really good homily that helped you see life in a new way or been moved by a religious talk on a retreat to make some really important changes in your life? Christians often call these spiritual moments "mountain top experiences," times of increased awareness of God and desire to follow God's will more faithfully.

Many of those who heard Jesus during the Sermon on the Mount had this same type of "mountain top experience." They began to see the Law of Moses differently because Jesus went beyond the letter of the Law to shed light on the spirit of the Law. This traveling rabbi also taught with a new kind of authority that empowered those with an open heart to experience the Kingdom of God that Jesus preached.

The Kingdom of God can, in a certain sense, be understood as the activity of God in our lives and the experience of conversion and personal knowledge of God that leads one to a new way of life making God's presence and love visible. Through the real presence of Jesus in the Word and Eucharist and the indwelling of the Holy Spirit we received at Baptism, we have access to that same life-changing power that Jesus proclaimed about the kingdom in the Sermon on the Mount.

Salesian Concept
Choosing the Best Virtues

Salesian Spirituality highlights the importance of our interior attitudes while performing external religious acts. This is not to say that physical actions are not important, but that without the right attitude, our virtuous practices can become empty rituals.

In the *Introduction to the Devout Life*, Saint Francis de Sales gives us some very important advice about what is most valuable to God concerning the practice of virtue. De Sales states, **"Concerning those virtues pertaining to our duties of state** (in life), **preference must be given to those** (virtues) **that are most excellent, not those which may be the most showy** ... **Thus it often happens that there is greater appreciation for material alms than for spiritual alms, for great bodily mortification than for spiritual mortifications such as gentleness, kindness and modesty. Yet these latter virtues** (spiritual mortifications) **are in fact superior to the former."**[5]

Truly, which do you think has the greater value in God's eyes, our words of praise or the heartfelt love that motivates us to praise God?

MEDITATION: A SALESIAN METHOD
1. Shift Gears from School Work to Prayer

> a. Throw off all your concerns from the school day. *(Relax)*
> b. Read Matthew 5:1-11

"When Jesus saw the crowds, he went up the mountain, and after he had sat down, his disciples came to him. He began to teach them, saying: 'Blessed are the poor in spirit, for theirs is the kingdom of heaven. Blessed are they who mourn, for they will be comforted. Blessed are the meek, for they will inherit the land. Blessed are they who hunger for and thirst for righteousness, for they will be satisfied. Blessed are the merciful, for they will be shown mercy. Blessed are the pure of heart, for they will see God. Blessed are the peacemakers, for they will be called children of God. Blessed are they who are persecuted for the sake of righteousness, for theirs is the kingdom of heaven. Blessed are you when they insult you and persecute you and utter every kind of evil against you (falsely) because of me. Rejoice and be glad, for your reward will be great in heaven. Thus they persecuted the prophets who were before you."

2. Experience Face Time with God

> a. Ask for a deeper awareness of God's presence.
> b. Ask for God's inspiration to pray sincerely.

3. Visualize the Story *(Ponder the story's sights, sounds, tastes, smells and feelings.)*

Imagine that you were there when Jesus went up the mountain to give the Beatitudes. You see Jesus' disciples among the crowd of Jews from Galilee and Judea. As Jesus preaches from the mountain top you hear people in the crowd say, "This is just like Moses." Another disagrees saying, "No, Moses was given the Commandments directly from God. This Jesus is speaking on his own authority. Not once did he say, 'Thus says the Lord!' like Moses and the prophets used to say." What is their reaction to all this? What is yours? Is your heart open to Jesus' teaching?

Jesus proclaims beatitudes for the poor in spirit, the mourning, and the persecuted. How do these beatitudes show that Jesus' Kingdom will require people to change both their actions and their attitudes? What changes of heart will you have to make to help these often neglected people? Do you believe Jesus has the authority to ask you to do these things?

Jesus reveals that the actual signs that the Kingdom of God is overcoming the Reign of Sin and Evil are that the mourning will receive comfort, the merciful will be shown mercy, the meek and gentle will inherit the earth and peacemakers will be called sons and daughters of God. How do these beatitudes set forth a plan of heartfelt actions that should mark the priorities of Christians everywhere?

Jesus states that those who hunger and thirst for righteousness will be satisfied and the pure of heart will see God. How do these Beatitudes illustrate how the Kingdom of God begins with an interior conversion that eventually changes the world one person at a time?

As you are about to leave you encounter Jesus. What to do want to say to him? What more does Jesus say to you about life?

4. Express Your Heart *(Write a three sentence spontaneous, heartfelt prayer.)*

What do you feel as you hear and see Jesus, the Eschatological Prophet, announcing the Kingdom of God by way of the Beatitudes? What can you say to Jesus to ask for the understanding and strength to live by the interior virtues expressed in the Beatitudes?

5. Be the Change *(Write a resolution that describes what you will do and when.)*

What do you feel you should do in order to live this day well in light of your meditation? Write one concrete resolution that can serve as your response to live according to the vision of the Beatitudes.

6. Text a Phrase *(Sum up your meditation into a text of around a 100 characters.)*

State within the confines of this spiritual journal the most helpful insight from your meditation. It can come from the Background, the Salesian Concept or your Salesian Meditation.

7. Create Word Art *(Express your text with visual art, poetry, music, or drama.)*

Express your Text a Phrase in a creative way that will help you recall your meditation with God throughout this day. Your art should help you strive for the most excellent interior virtues rather than just the most showy ones.

See the color icon for Christ the Teacher on page 90.

Visualize the Story *(Write down your insights about God from this meditation.)*

_____

_____

_____

_____

_____

_____

_____

_____

_____

_____

_____

_____

_____

_____

Express Your Heart *(Write a three sentence spontaneous, heartfelt prayer.)*

_____

_____

_____

_____

_____

_____

Be the Change *(Write a resolution that describes what you will do and when.)*

_____

_____

_____

Text a Phrase: *(Sum up your meditation into a text of around a 100 characters.)*

_____

_____

Create Word Art *(Express your text with visual art, poetry, music, or drama.)*

Christ the
Healer

Mark 2:1-12

Also
the Lamb of God
(John 1:29-34)

Background

Have you ever withheld helpful advice because you were afraid of what might happen? Maybe you had to tell an angry friend that he or she should really apologize for his/her part in a conflict. Maybe you were hesitant to give directions to a lost stranger because it would take you away from what you were doing at the moment. Whatever it was, you recognized the truth that helping others always involves a risk.

The paralytic's friends risked ridicule by suggesting that Jesus of Nazareth could cure paralysis. Jesus, the Lamb of God, who takes away the sins of the world, risked being accused of blasphemy by the scribes by forgiving sins. Jesus forgave the paralytic's sins to respond to an ancient Jewish belief that personal suffering was due to one's sin.

We often meet people who could benefit from a message in God's Word or from the healing found in the sacraments of Anointing and Reconciliation. While none of us wants to sound preachy, what good is faith in God if we never take advantage of it or share it with others?

People ask, "Does God still cure people today?" During the papacy of Pope John Paul II, there were over 200 newly canonized saints. This means that there were at least 200 confirmed miracles in 30 years. So while the Sacrament of Anointing does not always provide physical healing, there have been many times recently when it actually did more than just strengthen people to accept their suffering as Christ did.

Salesian Concept
Caring for the Sick and Suffering

While Saint Francis de Sales is best known for spiritual advice, he often took time to help the sick and suffering through ordinary acts of charity and by offering the sacraments along with his prayers for them. De Sales also taught catechism to a deaf boy by creating a simple sign language. He also originally founded the Visitation Sisters of Holy Mary, along with Saint Jane de Chantal, to care for the poor and sick.

Saint Francis took time himself to visit the sick in order to bring them the Sacraments of Reconciliation and Anointing of the Sick. Elizabeth Stopp's book, *Saint Francis de Sales: A Testimony by Saint Chantal*, states, **"Practically everyone who was ill begged for him** (De Sales) **to come and give them his blessing... this blessing would either cure outright or else help bring about a speedy and happy death."**[6]

MEDITATION: A SALESIAN METHOD

1. Shift Gears from School Work to Prayer

    a. Throw off all your concerns from the school day. *(Relax)*

    b. Read Mark 2:1-12

When Jesus returned to Capernaum after some days, it became known that he was at home. Many gathered together so that there was no longer room for them, not even around the door, and he preached the word to them. They came bringing to him a paralytic carried by four men. Unable to get near Jesus because of the crowd, they opened up the roof above him. After they had broken through, they let down the mat on which the paralytic was lying. When Jesus saw their faith, he said to the paralytic, "Child, your sins are forgiven." Now some of the scribes were sitting there asking themselves, "Why does this man speak that way? He is blaspheming. Who but God alone can forgive sins?" Jesus immediately knew in his mind what they were thinking to themselves, so he said, "Why are you thinking such things in your hearts? Which is easier, to say to the paralytic, 'Your sins are forgiven,' or to say, 'Rise, pick up your mat and walk?' But that you may know that the Son of Man has authority to forgive sins on earth"-- he said to the paralytic, "I say to you, rise, pick up your mat, and go home." He rose, picked up his mat at once, and went away in the sight of everyone. They were all astounded and glorified God, saying, "We have never seen anything like this."

2. Experience Face Time with God

    a. Ask for a deeper awareness of God's presence.

    b. Ask for God's inspiration to pray sincerely.

3. Visualize the Story *(Ponder the story's sights, sounds, tastes, smells and feelings.)*

    Imagine that you are the best friend of the paralytic in this story. You have heard people talking about this Jesus from Nazareth, a carpenter by trade, who is now preaching about the coming of the Kingdom of God. Could he be the one, the Messiah, the final prophet who is to come? What are you hoping to hear and see?

    After finally convincing your paralyzed friend to go to see Jesus, the large crowd prevents you from getting in once you arrive. Someone suggests lifting your friend up and lowering him through the roof. Why are you willing to risk such a dangerous stunt? What do you say to your friend to get him to give this a try? What does the excitement of the crowd say about Jesus and his ministry?

When you finally reach Jesus, he looks at you and your paralyzed friend. Seeing your faith and the expectation of the crowd, Jesus tells him, *"Child, your sins are forgiven."* Immediately some scribes protest saying, *"Only God can forgive sins."* What are you feeling now? What is the crowd's response to these scribes: silent support or angry murmurs? Whom do you believe, Jesus or these scribes?

Surprisingly, after rebuking these scribes, Jesus commands your friend, *"Rise, pick up your mat and walk."* As you see your friend take a deep breath, the desire of his heart to walk again renews the strength in his arms and legs. As he slowly rises to his feet, you first hear silence in the crowd. It is soon followed by resounding cheers as he begins to walk towards Jesus. What do you say and do as he reaches Jesus? Jesus smiles at you while hugging your friend. What do you believe about Jesus now?

4. Express Your Heart *(Write a three sentence spontaneous, heartfelt prayer.)*

What are you feeling as you walk home with your friend? What can you say to God for all the miraculous cures he has worked during Jesus' ministry and the miracles that continue today in the lives of the faithful? What can you say for the times you doubted Jesus' ability to heal or failed to lead your friends to Christ due to fear of ridicule?

5. Be the Change *(Write a resolution that describes what you will do and when.)*

What do you feel you should do in order to live this day well in light of your meditation? Write one concrete resolution that can serve as your response to believe in the healing power of Jesus in the sacraments.

6. Text a Phrase *(Sum up your meditation into a text of around a 100 characters.)*

State within the confines of this spiritual journal the most helpful insight from your meditation. It can come from the Background, the Salesian Concept or your Salesian Meditation.

7. Create Word Art *(Express your text with visual art, poetry, music, or drama.)*

Express your Text a Phrase in a creative way that will help you recall your meditation with God throughout this day. Your art should help you believe in the healing presence of God in your life and in the lives of others you know.

31

"The Spirit of the Lord God is upon me, because the Lord has anointed me. He has sent me to bring glad tidings to the lowly, to heal the brokenhearted, to proclaim liberty to captives and release to prisoners, to announce a year of favor from the Lord and a day of vindication by our God to comfort all who mourn."

Isaiah 61:1-2

"I say to you rise, pick up your mat and go home."

Mark 2:11

See the color icon for Christ the Healer on page 91.

Visualize the Story *(Write down your insights about God from this meditation.)*

_____

_____

_____

_____

_____

_____

_____

_____

_____

_____

_____

_____

_____

_____

Express Your Heart *(Write a three sentence spontaneous, heartfelt prayer.)*

_____

_____

_____

_____

_____

_____

Be the Change *(Write a resolution that describes what you will do and when.)*

_____

_____

_____

Text a Phrase: *(Sum up your meditation into a text of around a 100 characters.)*

_____

_____

Create Word Art *(Express your text with visual art, poetry, music, or drama.)*

Christ the Storyteller

Luke 16:19-31

"Upon those who dwelt in the land of gloom a light has shone."
Isaiah 9:1

Also the Light of the World (John 8:12-17) and The Way, the Truth and the Life (John 14:6)

Background

What do you think of word problems in math class? Do you love the challenge of figuring the essential concepts to solve the problem, or do you wish you could just be given a simple equation? Math teachers know that life does not come to us in simple equations, so they use word problems to help us discern whether or not we really understand the mathematical principles and concepts that are part of everyday life.

Jesus used parables like the Rich Man and Lazarus to see who was allowing his teachings to take root in their hearts. In the Beatitudes Jesus announced the Kingdom of God. Through his miracles, Jesus showed that the Kingdom of God was overcoming the reign of sin and evil and its grip on the world. Now, in his parables Jesus was seeing if his disciples were truly understanding the true meaning of his ministry. Jesus' parables are not mere stories. They are a radical call to embrace the demands of discipleship by accepting a new vision of life.

As the Way, the Truth and the Life (John 14:6), Jesus demands that we learn of his ways to find the truth and gain eternal life. As the Light of the World (John 8:12), Jesus gives us chances to grasp God's will in our complex world. May the Spirit of God open our hearts and minds to Jesus' teachings on how to do the will of God the Father in our lives.

Salesian Concept
What Does It Mean to
Love God and the Poor?

In the parable of the Rich Man and Lazarus, the rich man failed to understand the warnings of Moses and prophets against ignoring the needs of the poor and less fortunate. He allowed a large chasm in social economic status to keep him from meeting the needs of a poor man just outside his home. May Jesus' parable keep us from doing the same.

Saint Francis de Sales takes heed of this lesson from the parable of the Rich Man and Lazarus. He urges us to close the gap between us and the poor in our midst in the *Introduction to the Devout Life*, **"If you love the poor, Philothea, truly share their poverty and be poor like them. Seek their company, taking pleasure in welcoming them in your home, in visiting with them in theirs. Be at ease with them when you meet in church or on the street. Be poor in your speech when talking with them as a friend, but be rich with your hands by sharing with them what you have in greater abundance."[7]**

MEDITATION: A SALESIAN METHOD

1. Shift Gears from School Work to Prayer

a. Throw off all your concerns from the school day. *(Relax)*

b. Read Luke 16:19-31.

"There was a rich man who dressed in purple garments and fine linen and dined sumptuously each day. And lying at his door was a poor man named Lazarus, covered with sores, who would gladly have eaten his fill of the scraps that fell from the rich man's table. Dogs even used to come and lick his sores. When the poor man died, he was carried away by angels to the bosom of Abraham. The rich man also died and was buried, and from the netherworld, where he was in torment, he raised his eyes and saw Abraham far off and Lazarus at his side. And he cried out, 'Father Abraham, have pity on me. Send Lazarus to dip the tip of his finger in water and cool my tongue, for I am suffering torment in these flames.' Abraham replied, 'My child, remember that you received what was good during your lifetime while Lazarus likewise received what was bad; but now he is comforted here, whereas you are tormented. Moreover, between us and you a great chasm is established to prevent anyone from crossing who might wish to go from our side to yours or from your side to ours.' He said, 'Then I beg you, father, send him to my father's house, for I have five brothers, so that he may warn them, lest they too come to this place of torment.' But Abraham replied, 'They have Moses and the prophets. Let them listen to them.' He said, 'Oh no, father Abraham, but if someone from the dead goes to them, they will repent.' Then Abraham said, 'If they will not listen to Moses and the prophets, neither will they be persuaded if someone should rise from the dead.'"

2. Experience Face Time with God

a. Ask for a deeper awareness of God's presence.

b. Ask for God's inspiration to pray sincerely.

3. Visualize the Story *(Ponder the story's sights, sounds, tastes, smells and feelings.)*

Imagine that you are listening to the beginning of this parable of Jesus without knowing the end. Upon hearing the description of the rich man, you cannot help but wish that you too could dress like an aristocrat and eat like a king. In what other ways do you wish that your life today reflected the rich man in this parable? In what ways are you thankful that you do not live like Lazarus?

You pity Lazarus in comparison to the rich man's lifestyle, but other than seeing the two men as neighbors, what other connections do you see between them? In reality, what responsibilities do you feel the rich man has towards Lazarus based upon your own lived experience?

As a first century Palestinian Jew, it does not surprise you that Lazarus is in heaven. You are surprised, however, that the rich man is not in heaven. It is not until you hear that the rich man expects Abraham and Lazarus to immediately jump at his commands that you see the real problem. The rich man expects everything to go his way, revealing his arrogance. Lazarus, as part of God's Anawim, accepts both blessings and hardships with gratitude or patience along with an overall trust in God. Which description best matches your personality?

Jesus' parable ends with Abraham rejecting the rich man's last request to send someone back from the dead to warn his family. What do you make of Jesus' "word problem" that if they do not listen to Moses and the prophets, they will not be persuaded if someone should rise from the dead? What is the hidden message for Christians today?

4. Express Your Heart *(Write a three sentence spontaneous, heartfelt prayer.)*

What do you feel as you see the gap between the rich and the poor in the parable and in our world today? What prayer can you offer to God in order to show your desire to help the less fortunate even while enjoying the many gifts God has given to you and your family?

5. Be the Change *(Write a resolution that describes what you will do and when.)*

What do you feel you should do in order to live this day well in light of your meditation? Write one concrete resolution that can serve as your response to bridge the gap between the rich and the poor.

6. Text a Phrase *(Sum up your meditation into a text of around a 100 characters.)*

State within the confines of this spiritual journal the most helpful insight from your meditation. It can come from the Background, the Salesian Concept or your Salesian Meditation.

7. Create Word Art *(Express your text with visual art, poetry, music, or drama.)*

Express your Text a Phrase in a creative way that will help you recall your meditation with God throughout this day. Your art should help you reach out in order to get to know the poor among us and meet their needs.

"The people who walked in darkness have seen a great light; Upon those who dwelt in the land of gloom a light has shone."
Isaiah 9:1

See the color icon for Christ the Storyteller on page 91.

Visualize the Story *(Write down your insights about God from this meditation.)*

_____

_____

_____

_____

_____

_____

_____

_____

_____

_____

_____

_____

_____

_____

Express Your Heart *(Write a three sentence spontaneous, heartfelt prayer.)*

_____

_____

_____

_____

_____

_____

Be the Change *(Write a resolution that describes what you will do and when.)*

_____

_____

_____

Text a Phrase: *(Sum up your meditation into a text of around a 100 characters.)*

_____

_____

Create Word Art *(Express your text with visual art, poetry, music, or drama.)*

Christ the Humble Servant

John 13:1-2,4-17

Also the Teacher and Rabbi
(John 8:12-17)

Background

How do you feel about Christian Service Programs or the service hours required for Confirmation? Do you always choose the easiest way to meet the required hours? Do you refuse to do hard work or lowly tasks like cleaning stubborn rust stains from toilets? If not, then you already know that humbly serving others is the most concrete way we can follow Jesus' teaching to love our neighbors, especially the poor.

Think about your favorite subjects in school and the teachers who inspired you to love them. These teachers did more than just teach useful information and valuable insights about life. They used their imaginations to make hard-to-grasp concepts understandable. They modeled what they taught and invited you to join them in the challenge of learning what is truly important in life. As a rabbi or teacher of the Law, Jesus was all this and more to his closest followers.

At the Last Supper Jesus taught the Apostles a clear lesson about the value of service. Jesus modeled the humble service and love his followers would need to make his message accepted throughout the world. Jesus did this by washing the feet of his Apostles. This was a task befitting a slave or a very small child, but surely not a teacher of the Law. Yet, Jesus willingly did this as an example for us to follow. He also told the Apostles that all those who imitate his example of humble service were truly his friends. What new meaning does Jesus' washing his Apostles' feet give to your vision of service?

Salesian Concept
Roles in the Church

Even though Saint Francis de Sales was the Bishop of Geneva he took great satisfaction in acts of humble service on behalf of the poor. Elizabeth Stopp's book, *Saint Francis de Sales: A Testimony by Saint Chantal*, states that Saint Francis regularly gave the poor the clothes off his back and at least on one occasion gave the shoes from his feet. [8]

As you know De Sales had a great love for humility based upon the image of the humble and gentle Jesus from Matthew 11:29. This love for humble service is reflected in the *Introduction to the Devout Life*: "**The King of Glory, Philothea, does not reward His servants according to the dignity of the offices they hold, but according to the love and humility with which they fulfill them. It was while searching for the asses which had gone astray that Saul found his royal dignity.**"[9]

41

MEDITATION: A SALESIAN METHOD

1. Shift Gears from School Work to Prayer

a. Throw off all your concerns from the school day. *(Relax)*

b. Read John 13:1-2, 4-17

Before the feast of Passover, Jesus knew that his hour had come to pass from this world to the Father. He loved his own in the world and he loved them to the end. He rose from supper and took off his outer garments. He took a towel and tied it around his waist. Then he poured water into a basin and began to wash the disciples' feet and dry them with the towel around his waist. He came to Simon Peter, who said to him, "Master, are you going to wash my feet?" Jesus answered and said to him, "What I am doing, you do not understand now, but you will understand later." Peter said to him, "You will never wash my feet." Jesus answered him, "Unless I wash you, you will have no inheritance with me." Simon Peter said to him, "Master, then not only my feet, but my hands and head as well." Jesus said to him, "Whoever has bathed has no need except to have his feet washed, for he is clean all over; so you are clean, but not all." For he knew who would betray him; for this reason, he said, "Not all of you are clean."

So when he had washed their feet (and) put his garments back on and reclined at table again, he said to them, "Do you realize what I have done for you? You call me 'teacher' and 'master,' and rightly so, for indeed I am. If I, therefore, the master and teacher, have washed your feet, you ought to wash one another's feet. I have given you a model to follow, so that as I have done for you, you should also do. Amen, amen, I say to you, no slave is greater than his master nor any messenger greater than the one who sent him. If you understand this, blessed are you if you do it."

2. Experience Face Time with God

a. Ask for a deeper awareness of God's presence.

b. Ask for God's inspiration to pray sincerely.

3. Visualize the Story *(Ponder the story's sights, sounds, tastes, smells and feelings.)*

Imagine you are with Jesus at Passover. Jesus has just said that the unleavened bread was his body and the Passover wine was his blood. Jesus now rises from the table at which you have all been reclining to retrieve a pitcher of water and a basin. He then ties a towel around his waist. What are the Apostles saying to each other about it?

Jesus comes to Peter. At first Peter refuses to have his feet washed by Jesus. What is the expression on Jesus' face? What is the expression on Peter's face after Jesus rebukes not only his first refusal, but also his later request to wash his hands and head as well? Do you sense anything significant in the interaction between Peter and Jesus?

Jesus comes to wash your feet next. What does it look like to see Jesus at your feet? What sounds do you hear as Jesus pours water on your feet? How does it feel to have Jesus rub dirt off your feet and then dry your feet with a towel?

Finally, Jesus explains that he has given you all a model to follow. If he as teacher and master has washed your feet, you are called to that same humility if you want a share in Jesus' inheritance. How does Jesus' act of humility foreshadow his death on Calvary's cross?

4. Express Your Heart *(Write a three sentence spontaneous, heartfelt prayer.)*

What are you feeling as you hear Jesus say, *"Blessed are you if you do this"* referring to his example of humble service? What can you say to Jesus in response to his great humility and love? What attitudes do you have to change to be humble like Jesus in your service to others?

5. Be the Change *(Write a resolution that describes what you will do and when.)*

What do you feel you should do in order to live this day well in light of your meditation? Write one concrete resolution that can serve as your response to be more willing to serve where the need is the greatest no matter how inconvenient or belittling the task may be.

6. Text a Phrase *(Sum up your meditation into a text of around a 100 characters.)*

State within the confines of this spiritual journal the most helpful insight from your meditation. It can come from the Background, the Salesian Concept or your Salesian Meditation.

7. Create Word Art *(Express your text with visual art, poetry, music, or drama.)*

Express your Text a Phrase in a creative way that will help you recall your meditation with God throughout this day. Your art should help you humbly serve others after Jesus' model of service in washing the Apostles' feet.

"Here is my servant whom I uphold, my chosen one with whom I am pleased, Upon whom I have put my spirit; he shall bring forth justice to the nations, Not crying out, not shouting, not making his voice heard in the street. A bruised reed he shall not break, and a smoldering wick he shall not quench, until he establishes justice on the earth."

Isaiah 42:1-4a

See the color icon for Christ the Humble Servant on page 92.

Visualize the Story *(Write down your insights about God from this meditation.)*

_____

_____

_____

_____

_____

_____

_____

_____

_____

_____

_____

_____

_____

_____

_____

Express Your Heart *(Write a three sentence spontaneous, heartfelt prayer.)*

_____

_____

_____

_____

_____

_____

Be the Change *(Write a resolution that describes what you will do and when.)*

_____

_____

_____

Text a Phrase: *(Sum up your meditation into a text of around a 100 characters.)*

_____

_____

Create Word Art *(Express your text with visual art, poetry, music, or drama.)*

Christ the Suffering Servant

Mark 14:32-42

Also the Rock
Matthew 7:21-27

Background

How do you think you would respond if you ever faced death? Would you face it calmly or would you be anxious with fear? Would you think about saving yourself or would you think of others?

Throughout the Passion Narratives we see Jesus suffering greatly. If we look very closely, we will also see Jesus focusing mainly on God and others. At his arrest in the Garden, he healed the servant who had his ear cut off. While carrying the cross, he told the women to weep for themselves and their children, rather than for him. Even on the Cross, Jesus had compassion for the Good Thief and forgiveness for those who crucified him. Jesus died as he lived, as a servant for God and others.

As God's Suffering Servant and our Rock (see Matthew 7:21-27), Jesus placed his full confidence in God in even the darkest times. Jesus knew that even death could not stop God's plan to free everyone from the grasp of sin and death. It is important to know that while Jesus died for love of God, he also died particularly for love of you.

Salesian Concept
The Thought of Death on the Top of the Hour

In the *Introduction to the Devout Life* Saint Francis tells us to plan to do everything we can to prepare for our last hour on earth. He rightly points out that the things we often value in life, such as wealth and popularity, will appear as worthless as sand at the moment of our death. De Sales states, **"Devotion and good works will appear delightful, and you will regret having practiced them so little... May the certitude of your death incite you to cast yourself into God's arms with great confidence, beseeching Him to let your whole life be sorrow, if your death be good** (ending in resurrection). **Resolve not to set your heart on this world, even on friends and relatives, except to love them with a holy love that will last in eternity."**[10]

To do this Saint Francis would think about death as the bells tolled at the top of every hour. De Sales did this not to scare himself into being good, but just to help him unite his will to the will of God, as Jesus did throughout his life. Thus, even if he was practicing his sword fighting skills or riding his horse, rather than running for the nearest church, he would simply remind himself that he was made to spend eternity with God. Thus, he could grow closer to God while enjoying what he was doing at the moment. Let us try to do the same every hour of our lives.

MEDITATION: A SALESIAN METHOD

1. Shift Gears from School Work to Prayer

    a. Throw off all your concerns from the school day. *(Relax)*
    b. Read Mark 14:32-42.

Then they came to a place named Gethsemane, and he (Jesus) said to his disciples, "Sit here while I pray." He took with him Peter, James, and John, and began to be troubled and distressed. Then he said to them, "My soul is sorrowful even to death. Remain here and keep watch." He advanced a little and fell to the ground and prayed that if it were possible the hour might pass by him; he said, "Abba, Father, all things are possible to you. Take this cup away from me, but not what I will but what you will." When he returned he found them asleep. He said to Peter, "Simon, are you asleep? Could you not keep watch for one hour? Watch and pray that you may not undergo the test. The spirit is willing but the flesh is weak." Withdrawing again, he prayed, saying the same thing. Then he returned once more and found them asleep, for they could not keep their eyes open and did not know what to answer him. He returned a third time and said to them, "Are you still sleeping and taking your rest? It is enough. The hour has come. Behold, the Son of Man is to be handed over to sinners. Get up, let us go. See, my betrayer is at hand."

2. Experience Face Time with God

    a. Ask for a deeper awareness of God's presence.
    b. Ask for God's inspiration to pray sincerely.

3. Visualize the Story *(Ponder the story's sights, sounds, tastes, smells and feelings.)*

    Imagine that your mother has told you where Jesus and his disciples were eating their Passover Meal. You have heard much about Jesus, but the crowds have been so large that you could not get as close to Jesus as you had wished. What do you want to ask Jesus if you get the chance?

    Now, as Jesus and his disciples leave the Upper Room, you start to follow them as they sing traditional Passover songs recalling God's powerful deeds to free the Hebrews from slavery in Egypt. What is the mood of the disciples as they sing these songs?

    As they enter the Garden of Gethsemane, you can see that you are really alone with Jesus and his Apostles. How excited are you at finally being able to see Jesus up close and perhaps talk to him?

Just before you get close enough to call out to Jesus, you hear Jesus tell his disciples that he is sorrowful to the point of death. Why is this a shock to you in view of Jesus' popularity with the people?

After he takes Peter, James and John with him, Jesus falls to the ground and prays. You hear him call out to God as *"Abba"* as he asks that his cup of suffering be taken from him, if it is the Father's will. What is Jesus' facial expression? What is the tone of his voice?

When Jesus returns from prayer three times to find his closest friends sleeping, what emotions fill your heart? To what extent do you experience the truth of Jesus' statement, *"The spirit is willing but the flesh is weak"* in your walk of faith? What sense of love do you see in Jesus' wish that his friends be spared from the test he will soon face?

Finally, as Jesus sees his betrayal is about to happen, what level of courage and love do you see in his expression and body language? What do you see in Jesus that reflects his trust in God and love for you?

4. Express Your Heart *(Write a three sentence spontaneous, heartfelt prayer.)*

What are you feeling as you see Jesus place his trust in God during a time of great distress without the support of his friends? What can you say to Jesus as a pledge to remain united to him in prayer?

5. Be the Change *(Write a resolution that describes what you will do and when.)*

What do you feel you should do in order to live this day well in light of your meditation? Write one concrete resolution that can help you to follow Jesus' courageous example of trust despite being overwhelmed with fear. How could you live for love of Christ, who died for love of you?

6. Text a Phrase *(Sum up your meditation into a text of around a 100 characters.)*

State within the confines of this spiritual journal the most helpful insight from your meditation. It can come from the Background, the Salesian Concept or your Salesian Meditation.

7. Create Word Art *(Express your text with visual art, poetry, music, or drama.)*

Express your Text a Phrase in a creative way that will help you recall your meditation with God throughout this day. Your art should help you live according to God's will with an eye to sharing eternity with God.

"Because he surrendered himself to death and was counted among the wicked; and he shall take away the sins of many and win pardon for their offenses." Isaiah 53:12

See the color icon for Christ the Suffering Servant on page 92.

Visualize the Story *(Write down your insights about God from this meditation.)*

_____

_____

_____

_____

_____

_____

_____

_____

_____

_____

_____

_____

_____

_____

_____

_____

Express Your Heart *(Write a three sentence spontaneous, heartfelt prayer.)*

_____

_____

_____

_____

_____

_____

Be the Change *(Write a resolution that describes what you will do and when.)*

_____

_____

_____

Text a Phrase: *(Sum up your meditation into a text of around a 100 characters.)*

_____

_____

Create Word Art *(Express your text with visual art, poetry, music, or drama.)*

Christ Our Redeemer

John 19:16-18, 25-30

Also the Good Shepherd
(John 10:1-18)

Background

Do you have the same love for the Church as you do for Jesus? Though people should respond affirmatively to that question, many people today might not say "yes" to it. Two recent books, *The Shack* and *They Love Jesus, but Hate the Church* express this modern phenomenon. No matter where you fall on the love of Jesus / love of Church scale, this meditation is for you.

Our story about the Crucifixion focuses upon Jesus' closest followers, Mary, the Mother of God, and John, the Beloved. Mary models the essential traits that all Christians in the Church are meant to exhibit. She loves Jesus with perfect devotion and imitates Jesus' love and forgiveness towards all, even people who hurt or totally reject Jesus. John the Beloved highlights that even after we fail to live up to all that friendship in Christ entails, Jesus is always ready to forgive us. As our Redeemer, Jesus makes up for our sinfulness and renews our broken relationship with God through his perfect obedience and sacrifice. Jesus, as the Good Shepherd, calls us all to be in a loving relationship with one another based upon our relationship with him.

Therefore, it is not we, the members of the Church, that are perfect, but rather Jesus, who perfects us into the one family of God.

Salesian Concept
Love of the Church

Many people today paint the Church as a human institution with inconvenient rules and stern judgments. The teachings of Saint Francis de Sales can help us appreciate the Church more as our spiritual family and home rather than by that false image. De Sales teaches that next to the love of our Lord, we should love the Church.[11] While De Sales had a great devotion to the Church as the Bride of Christ, he was not blind to the mistakes we all make while professing to represent the Church.

In *The Catholic Controversy* Francis wrote, **"Our Lord had in his humanity two parts, body and soul; so the Church his spouse has two parts, the interior which is as her soul, invisible - Faith, Hope, Charity and Grace, - the other exterior, as her body, visible... Its greatest beauty is within, the outside is not so excellent."**[12]

De Sales teaches us that the chief characteristic of our love for others is putting up with their shortcomings. Thus, loving others in the Church despite their failings is the best way to imitate Christ's love for us. Therefore, let us love the Church to show our true love for Christ.

MEDITATION: A SALESIAN METHOD

1. Shift Gears from School Work to Prayer

a. Throw off all your concerns from the school day. *(Relax)*

b. Read John 19:16-18, 25-30

Then he (Pontius Pilate) handed him (Jesus) over to them to be crucified. So they took Jesus, and carrying the cross himself he went out to what is called the Place of the Skull, in Hebrew, Golgotha. There they crucified him, and with him two others, one on either side, with Jesus in the middle....

Standing by the cross of Jesus were his mother and his mother's sister, Mary the wife of Clopas, and Mary of Magdala. When Jesus saw his mother and the disciple there whom he loved, he said to his mother, "Woman, behold, your son." Then he said to the disciple, "Behold, your mother." And from that hour the disciple took her into his home. After this, aware that everything was now finished, in order that the scripture might be fulfilled, Jesus said, "I thirst." There was a vessel filled with common wine. So they put a sponge soaked in wine on a sprig of hyssop and put it up to his mouth. When Jesus had taken the wine, he said, "It is finished." And bowing his head, he handed over the spirit.

2. Experience Face Time with God

a. Ask for a deeper awareness of God's presence.

b. Ask for God's inspiration to pray sincerely.

3. Visualize the Story *(Ponder the story's sights, sounds, tastes, smells and feelings.)*

Imagine that you are the youngest of the Twelve Apostles, John the Beloved. You have followed Jesus for three years. You recall your first memories of Jesus in Galilee: his calling you from the shore of the Sea, Jesus' many teachings about the Kingdom of God during the Sermon on the Mount, his healing and nature miracles and his intriguing parables. Which of these experiences mean the most to you now?

Your thoughts turn to your most recent days in Jerusalem: Jesus' entry into the city, Jesus' confrontation with the leaders of the Temple, the Last Super when Jesus offered a meal for a New Covenant, Jesus washing your feet and his arrest in the Garden when no one could stay awake and all abandoned him. What are your thoughts about each of these events? Do you see Jesus as a victim or as a prophet? Explain.

You have now been following Jesus from a distance as he carried his cross to Golgotha. It is an eerie place, made even more ominous by the darkness covering the afternoon sky. You are afraid to get too close or even to make eye contact with Jesus until you see Mary, his mother, at the foot of the Cross. What do you notice about Mary? What moves you to forget your fears and kneel next to her?

As you kneel next to Mary at the foot of the Cross, she takes your hand and looks lovingly into your eyes. This gives you the courage to finally look up at Jesus. As you do this, Jesus also looks at you with love. Then, Jesus says to Mary his mother, *"Woman, behold, your son."* Next, Jesus turns to you and says, *"Behold, your mother."* In what ways do you see Mary as Jesus' most faithful disciple? How does Mary symbolize the community of Jesus' closest followers?

Jesus says, *"I thirst"* quoting Psalm 22, that also states, *"And I will live for the Lord."* Jesus then states, *"It is finished."* as he hands over his spirit. What do make of all this as Mary sobs in your arms?

4. Express Your Heart *(Write a three sentence spontaneous, heartfelt prayer.)*

What am I feeling as I hear Mary crying for her Son and my friend Jesus? What can I say to God as my response to Christ dying for my shortcomings and sins?

5. Be the Change *(Write a resolution that describes what you will do and when.)*

What do you feel you should do in order to live this day well in light of your meditation? Write one concrete resolution that can help you show greater love for the other followers of Jesus, whom Christ has gathered into the Church as the Good Shepherd.

6. Text a Phrase *(Sum up your meditation into a text of around a 100 characters.)*

State within the confines of this spiritual journal the most helpful insight from your meditation. It can come from the Background, the Salesian Concept or your Salesian Meditation.

7. Create Word Art *(Express your text with visual art, poetry, music, or drama.)*

Express your Text a Phrase in a creative way that will help you recall your meditation with God throughout this day. Your art should help you love all those Christ has redeemed despite their many failings.

Upon him was the chastisement that makes us whole, by his stripes we were healed... We had all gone astray like sheep, each following his own ways but the Lord laid upon him the guilt of us all.
Isaiah 53:5b-6

"Woman, behold your son."
"Behold, your mother."

See the color icon for Christ our Redeemer on page 93.

Visualize the Story *(Write down your insights about God from this meditation.)*

_____

_____

_____

_____

_____

_____

_____

_____

_____

_____

_____

_____

_____

_____

Express Your Heart *(Write a three sentence spontaneous, heartfelt prayer.)*

_____

_____

_____

_____

_____

_____

Be the Change *(Write a resolution that describes what you will do and when.)*

_____

_____

_____

Text a Phrase: *(Sum up your meditation into a text of around a 100 characters.)*

_____

_____

Create Word Art *(Express your text with visual art, poetry, music, or drama.)*

The Risen Christ

Luke 24:13-18,25-35

Also the Son of God (Mark 1:1), The Bread of Life (John 6:1-71) and The Word of Life (1 John 1:1)

Background

What is your experience of going to Mass on Sundays or on special occasions in school or with your family? Do you go willingly or do you have to be dragged by the arm to go? After meditating on the story of the Disciples on the Road to Emmaus, perhaps you will appreciate the Mass more as an opportunity to experience the Risen Jesus.

All the major parts of the Mass are reflected in this Gospel story. Just as every Mass begins with the **Greeting**, so in our story the Risen Jesus greeted the disciples in the midst of their grief. In the same manner just as every **Penitential Rite** calls us to repent of our slowness of heart to believe and live in the joy of the Gospel, so Jesus had to call these disciples to task for not believing the words of the women who announced that Jesus was risen from the dead.

The **Liturgy of the Word** is reflected in Jesus' explanation of how both the Law and the Prophets testified that Jesus, as the Messiah, would have to suffer and die before being glorified by the Father. If our hearts are open to the presence of Jesus in the Scriptures, then our hearts will burn with devotion as the two disciples recalled later.

If we are fully attentive to the **Liturgy of the Eucharist**, which recalls the Last Supper and Jesus' sacrificial love, then we will be able to recognize the Risen Jesus in the Eucharist as the disciples did. Just as the story of the Disciples on the Road to Emmaus ends with them going out to share with the others how Jesus was made known to them in the breaking of the bread, so we, too, are sent out to love and serve the Lord and one another at the **Concluding Rite** of each Mass.

Salesian Concept
Receiving the Eucharist

In the *Introduction to the Devout Life* Saint Francis calls the Eucharist, "the sun of all spiritual exercises."[13] De Sales also states, "Prayer made in union with this divine Sacrifice has incalculable power."[14]

According to Saint Francis de Sales, "There are two kinds of people who ought to receive Holy Communion frequently: . . . the strong so that they may not become weak, and the weak so that they may become strong."[15] Finally, De Sales states "By virtue of adoring and eating Beauty, Goodness and Purity itself in this Divine Sacrament, you will become altogether beautiful, good and pure."[16]

MEDITATION: A SALESIAN METHOD

1. Shift Gears from School Work to Prayer

    a. Throw off all your concerns from the school day. *(Relax)*

    b. Read Luke 24:13-18, 25-35.

Now that very day two of them were going to a village seven miles from Jerusalem called Emmaus, and they were conversing about all the things that had occurred. And it happened that while they were conversing and debating, Jesus himself drew near and walked with them, but their eyes were prevented from recognizing him. He asked them, "What are you discussing as you walk along?" They stopped, looking downcast. One of them, named Cleopas, said to him in reply, "Are you the only visitor to Jerusalem who does not know of the things that have taken place there in these days?" And he replied to them, "What sort of things?" They said to him, "The things that happened to Jesus the Nazarene, who was a prophet mighty in deed and word before God and all the people, how our chief priests and rulers both handed him over to a sentence of death and crucified him..." And he said to them, "Oh, how foolish you are! How slow of heart to believe all that the prophets spoke! Was it not necessary that the Messiah should suffer these things and enter into his glory?" Then beginning with Moses and all the prophets, he interpreted to them what referred to him in all the scriptures. As they approached the village to which they were going, he gave the impression that he was going on farther. But they urged him, "Stay with us, for it is nearly evening and the day is almost over." So he went in to stay with them. And it happened that, while he was with them at table, he took bread, said the blessing, broke it, and gave it to them. With that their eyes were opened and they recognized him, but he vanished from their sight. Then they said to each other, "Were not our heart burning (within us) while he spoke to us on the way and opened the scriptures to us?" So they set out at once and returned to Jerusalem where they found gathered together the eleven and those with them who were saying, "The Lord has truly been raised and has appeared to Simon!" Then the two recounted what had taken place on the way and how he was made known to them in the breaking of the bread.

2. Experience Face Time with God

    a. Ask for a deeper awareness of God's presence.

    b. Ask for God's inspiration to pray sincerely.

3. Visualize the Story *(Ponder the story's sights, sounds, tastes, smells and feelings.)*

    Imagine you are the other disciple with Cleopas on the road to Emmaus retelling the events of Jesus' Passion and Death full of sorrow. The traveler listens to your story with sympathy, but then all of a sudden he turns around and calls you foolish. How does this make you feel? Angry? Embarrassed? Ashamed? Yet the more he speaks about the Law and the Prophets, the more you appreciate his wisdom. The traveler appears to be going farther as you reach the town of Emmaus. You yearn to hear to more of his insights about the Messiah, since you have not felt this level of joy and peace in your heart since the last time you heard Jesus preach. What is his facial expression as you both plead with him to continue his journey later and share a meal with you?

As you sit down at table, the traveler takes the bread, breaks it and blesses it in the exact manner that Jesus' did at the Last Supper. Suddenly, you realize this traveler is the very same Jesus, now risen from the dead. Before you can say a word, the Risen Jesus is gone, but the peace and joy that fill your heart remain as you rush back to Jerusalem with the Good News. What are you planning to say to the Apostles and other disciples about the wonder of the Risen Jesus?

4. Express Your Heart *(Write a three sentence spontaneous, heartfelt prayer.)*

What are you feeling as you rush to tell the Apostles about meeting the Risen Jesus? What can you say for the times you failed to recognize the presence of the Risen Jesus in the Eucharist and readings at Mass? What praise can you offer the Risen Jesus for giving you a share in his resurrection as well as his victory over sin and death?

5. Be the Change *(Write a resolution that describes what you will do and when.)*

What do you feel you should do in order to live this day well in light of your meditation? Write one concrete resolution that can help you live with Easter joy each day of the year.

6. Text a Phrase *(Sum up your meditation into a text of around a 100 characters.)*

State within the confines of this spiritual journal the most helpful insight from your meditation. It can come from the Background, the Salesian Concept or your Salesian Meditation.

7. Create Word Art *(Express your text with visual art, poetry, music, or drama.)*

Express your Text a Phrase in a creative way that will help you recall your meditation with God throughout this day. Your art should help you live out the meaning of the Resurrection of Christ not only on Sundays but throughout the entire week.

See the color icon for Christ Our Risen Savior on page 93.

Visualize the Story *(Write down your insights about God from this meditation.)*

_____

_____

_____

_____

_____

_____

_____

_____

_____

_____

_____

_____

_____

_____

_____

Express Your Heart *(Write a three sentence spontaneous, heartfelt prayer.)*

_____

_____

_____

_____

_____

_____

Be the Change *(Write a resolution that describes what you will do and when.)*

_____

_____

_____

Text a Phrase: *(Sum up your meditation into a text of around a 100 characters.)*

_____

_____

Create Word Art *(Express your text with visual art, poetry, music, or drama.)*

The Risen Christ Who Sends the Holy Spirit

Acts 2:1-13

Read about the Holy Spirit as Advocate and Helper (John 14:16)

Background

Have you ever been involved in a new group activity that others knew very little of, except that they now wanted a piece of the action? Recall your first experiences on Facebook or Twitter. Were you one of the first to get in on it or one of the last? Depending upon which, it will have an effect on your view of this story.

The Twelve Apostles were similarly gathered together with something new that would change the world. At first they were afraid to share it out of fear that their eye-witnessed accounts of Jesus' rising from the dead would get them in trouble with the authorities. All that fear vanished once the Holy Spirit descended upon Mary and the Apostles, who were Twelve again after choosing Matthias to replace Judas. The result was the birth of the Church that we know today.

The Holy Spirit empowered these first followers to fulfill the mission given to the Apostles by the Risen Jesus in Matthew 28:19-20: *"Go, therefore and make disciples of all nations, baptizing them in the name of the Father, and of the Son, and of the holy Spirit, teaching them to observe all I have commanded you. And behold I am with you always, until the end of the age."*

The Apostles needed to trust in the guidance of the Holy Spirit, in order to fulfill their world-changing mission from Christ. The Spirit led the Apostles in all truth about the meaning of Jesus and his teachings as their Advocate and Helper. We need to trust the Holy Spirit to help us share faith in Christ with others in meaningful ways.

Salesian Concept
Telling Others about Jesus

Saint Francis de Sales encourages us to overcome any fear we may have about witnessing to our faith in the Risen Christ by saying, **"If you truly love God, then you will speak about God at every real opportunity."**[17]

Rather than being like door to door preachers, Salesian Spirituality would have us focus upon our real opportunities to share our faith. First, audibly pray and sing the songs at Mass. Second, if a person ever asks why you have helped him, be sure to mention Christ, if you can do so sincerely. Third, if you become a parent, make sure that you share why you love God with your children and model that love for them.

MEDITATION: A SALESIAN METHOD

1. Shift Gears from School Work to Prayer

a. Throw off all your concerns from the school day. *(Relax)*

b. Read Acts 2:1-13 below.

When the time for Pentecost was fulfilled, they were all in one place together. And suddenly there came from the sky a noise like a strong driving wind, and it filled the entire house in which they were. Then there appeared to them tongues as of fire, which parted and came to rest on each one of them. And they were all filled with the holy Spirit and began to speak in different tongues, as the Spirit enabled them to proclaim. Now there were devout Jews from every nation under heaven staying in Jerusalem. At this sound, they gathered in a large crowd, but they were confused because each one heard them speaking in his own language. They were astounded, and in amazement they asked, "Are not all these people who are speaking Galileans? Then how does each of us hear them in his own native language? We are Parthians, Medes, and Elamites, inhabitants of Mesopotamia, Judea and Cappadocia, Pontus and Asia, Phrygia and Pamphylia, Egypt and the districts of Libya near Cyrene, as well as travelers from Rome, both Jews and converts to Judaism, Cretans and Arabs, yet we hear them speaking in our own tongues of the mighty acts of God." They were all astounded and bewildered, and said to one another, "What does this mean?" But others said, scoffing, "They have had too much new wine."

2. Experience Face Time with God

a. Ask for a deeper awareness of God's presence.

b. Ask for God's inspiration to pray sincerely.

3. Visualize the Story *(Ponder the story's sights, sounds, tastes, smells and feelings.)*

Imagine that you are Matthias, the newest member of the Twelve. You are with Peter, James, and John, and the other Apostles, who with Mary, Jesus' mother, are waiting for the Spirit that Jesus promised at the Last Supper. How does it feel to be one of the Twelve Apostles?

It is early on the morning of the Jewish Feast of Pentecost. You recall that Pentecost celebrates Israel's being given the Law of Moses and Israel's annual thanksgiving to God for the new harvest presented at the Temple. Why would today be a good day for the arrival of the Advocate and Helper the Risen Jesus promised?

Suddenly a strong wind fills the room with the glow from a flame that immediately separates and appears as tongues of fire over the heads of Mary and the Apostles. The gentle warmth of these flames removes everyone's fear as they are filled with love, joy, courage, knowledge and understanding. What is the expression on everyone's face? What does Mary say to encourage you? What does Peter say to inspire all of you to go out among the people?

As you all leave the room in which you were hiding, you see a great crowd of Jews gathered outside. How can you express to them that Jesus fulfilled the Law of Moses by his death and resurrection? How can you explain that Jesus sent the Holy Spirit as the first fruits of the resurrection for all those who believe in Jesus Christ?

As you begin to express these truths, something amazing happens. You suddenly realize that everyone can understand you no matter what language they speak. How is this a reversal of the story of Babel, as they begin to rejoice as one people in the mighty acts of God? Finally, you hear some people accusing you of being drunk. How does this show that sharing the Good News will not always be easy?

4. Express Your Heart *(Write a three sentence spontaneous, heartfelt prayer.)*

What are you feeling as you look out on all those people? What prayer can you offer to the Holy Spirit to give you the courage to joyfully share your knowledge and understanding of Christ to others?

5. Be the Change *(Write a resolution that describes what you will do and when.)*

What do you feel you should do in order to live this day well in light of your meditation? Write a concrete resolution to talk about Jesus at every real opportunity in terms of today's Salesian Concept.

6. Text a Phrase *(Sum up your meditation into a text of around a 100 characters.)*

State within the confines of this spiritual journal the most helpful insight from your meditation. It can come from the Background, the Salesian Concept or your Salesian Meditation.

7. Create Word Art *(Express your text with visual art, poetry, music, or drama.)*

Express your Text a Phrase in a creative way that will help you recall your meditation with God throughout this day. Your art should help you sincerely witness to your faith in Christ in public.

See the color icon for the Risen Christ Sends the Spirit on page 94.

Visualize the Story *(Write down your insights about God from this meditation.)*

_____

_____

_____

_____

_____

_____

_____

_____

_____

_____

_____

_____

_____

_____

Express Your Heart *(Write a three sentence spontaneous, heartfelt prayer.)*

_____

_____

_____

_____

_____

_____

Be the Change *(Write a resolution that describes what you will do and when.)*

_____

_____

_____

Text a Phrase: *(Sum up your meditation into a text of around a 100 characters.)*

_____

_____

Create Word Art *(Express your text with visual art, poetry, music, or drama.)*

Christ in Scripture and Tradition

1 Corinthians 15:1-11

Saul, Saul, why are you persecuting me?

Read the Crucified Risen One
Acts 2:22-36 and Acts 9:1-22

Background

If you have ever questioned the reliability of the stories about Jesus that you read in the Bible, this meditation is for you. Actually recent biblical archeology and historical research point to the reliability of the Bible as it has been handed down to us today. Let me explain.

The scribes, who copied the original scrolls of the Bible, practiced solemn prayer and purification rituals before they even started working. Afterwards, they would mathematically check their work by counting each word and letter and even making sure that the middle word and the middle letter of the copy matched the original text.

The book of Isaiah proves the accuracy of the Bible we use today. It laid undisturbed for 1900 years in a cave holding the *Dead Sea Scrolls*. These scrolls came from the Essenes, a monastic type of religious group that held to a very strict interpretation of the Jewish Law. Christians, on the other hand, were a new radical religious group that accepted both Jews and non-Jews. Now the New Testament quotes the prophet Isaiah more than any other source. If Christians or the Essenes changed the biblical text in favor of their beliefs, logic holds that both texts of Isaiah would be different from the Jewish text used today. In reality, all three texts match in substance. We should not be surprised by this, since we know that the Bible is not an ordinary book, but the Word of God written by human authors guided by the inspiration of the Holy Spirit.

Salesian Concept

The Scriptures and Apostolic Tradition

The last verse of John's Gospel highlights the importance of the experience of the Apostles from which the Gospels were written. John 21:25 states, *"There are many other things that Jesus did, but if these were to be described individually, I do not think the whole world would contain all the books that would be written."* This collective experience is called Apostolic Tradition. In the *Catholic Controversy,* De Sales taught **"Scripture** (*New Testament*) **itself is only Apostolic Tradition reduced to writing, with the infallible assistance of the Holy Spirit."**[18]

We call this on-going experience of the Church, Sacred Tradition, which De Sales identified as the "Rule of Faith." In the Catholic Church, Sacred Tradition is safeguarded by Apostolic Succession or the unbroken historical link between the Apostles and our current bishops today under the guidance of the Holy Spirit. Now this we can trust.

MEDITATION: A SALESIAN METHOD

1. Shift Gears from School Work to Prayer

a. Throw off all your concerns from the school day. *(Relax)*

b. Read 1 Corinthians 15:1-11 below.

Now I am reminding you, brothers, of the gospel I preached to you, which you indeed received and in which you also stand. Through it you are also being saved, if you hold fast to the word I preached to you, unless you believed in vain. For I handed on to you as of first importance what I also received: that Christ died for our sins in accordance with the scriptures; that he was buried; that he was raised on the third day in accordance with the scriptures; that he appeared to Cephas (Peter), then to the Twelve. After that, he appeared to more than five hundred brothers at once, most of whom are still living, though some have fallen asleep. After that he appeared to James, then to all the apostles. Last of all, as to one born abnormally, he appeared to me. For I am the least of the apostles, not fit to be called an apostle, because I persecuted the church of God. But by the grace of God I am what I am, and his grace to me has not been ineffective. Indeed, I have toiled harder than all of them; not I, however, but the grace of God (that is) with me. Therefore, whether it be I or they, so we preach and so you believed.

2. Experience Face Time with God

a. Ask for a deeper awareness of God's presence.

b. Ask for God's inspiration to pray sincerely.

3. Visualize the Story *(Ponder the story's sights, sounds, tastes, smells and feelings.)*

Imagine that you are Paul trying to write a letter in response to reports that certain members of the church at Corinth are doubting Jesus' bodily resurrection. Why is it so essential that they believe in the resurrection of the body based upon your experience?

As Greeks, they hold to the Socratic belief that the body is just a prison for the soul, keeping one from attaining truth. When they heard that Jesus rose in body, they were upset. So now you have decided to remind them of how they first came to believe in the Risen Jesus. You tell them that it was not through ordinary human words that they believed, but through the power of the Holy Spirit, who worked miraculous healings and signs among them. What signs of the Holy Spirit can you recall from the life of the early Church?

Knowing the Corinthians need more convincing, you explain how the Risen Jesus appeared first to Peter, then to the Twelve, then to 500 Christians at once, then to James and finally to you as you sought to arrest the followers of this Risen Jesus. While you can sympathize with their disbelief, how did your experience of the Risen Jesus on the road to Damascus become the basis of your current preaching that Christ did indeed rise in a body?

You humbly explain that you are not worthy to be an apostle, but by the grace of God you have been called to witness to Jews and Greeks alike about the Risen Jesus you encountered. How has your tireless work as an apostle (traveling by foot, enduring rejection and beatings in jail) been a sign of the power of God? Why is it important that your testimony of Jesus' resurrection match the one handed on by Peter and the Twelve?

4. Express Your Heart *(Write a three sentence spontaneous, heartfelt prayer.)*

What are you feeling as you finish the letter? What can you say to God to help you become a better witness to the power and truth behind Jesus' bodily resurrection that you hope to share?

5. Be the Change *(Write a resolution that describes what you will do and when.)*

What do you feel you should do in order to live this day well in light of your meditation? Write one concrete resolution to pass on what you have received, namely that Christ died for our sins and was raised on the third day in accordance with the Scriptures?

6. Text a Phrase *(Sum up your meditation into a text of around a 100 characters.)*

State within the confines of this spiritual journal the most helpful insight from your meditation. It can come from the Background, the Salesian Concept or your Salesian Meditation.

7. Create Word Art *(Express your text with visual art, poetry, music, or drama.)*

Express your Text a Phrase in a creative way that will help you recall your meditation with God throughout this day. Your art should help you stand firm in the faith handed on to us by the first Apostles through the Sacred Tradition of the Church. It should also help you place your trust in the Holy Spirit and Apostolic Succession.

See the color icon for Christ in Scripture and Tradition on page 94.

Visualize the Story *(Write down your insights about God from this meditation.)*

_____

_____

_____

_____

_____

_____

_____

_____

_____

_____

_____

_____

_____

_____

Express Your Heart *(Write a three sentence spontaneous, heartfelt prayer.)*

_____

_____

_____

_____

_____

_____

Be the Change *(Write a resolution that describes what you will do and when.)*

_____

_____

_____

Text a Phrase: *(Sum up your meditation into a text of around a 100 characters.)*

_____

_____

Create Word Art *(Express your text with visual art, poetry, music, or drama.)*

Jesus and Life in the Spirit

Romans 8:1-15

Read Jesus and the Spirit
Luke 10:21-24

Background

How do you view God's presence in your life? Is God a mere concept that you can simply reject based upon the lack of visible evidence? Or do you view God just as a set of moral laws associated with religion? Hopefully, you relate to God on a more personal level, having real gratitude for the many gifts you have received from the Father as your Creator, Jesus as your Redeemer and the Holy Spirit as your Sanctifier.

In the Letter to the Romans Saint Paul identifies the first two ways of relating to God as living according to the flesh, while the third way he calls living according to the spirit. Saint Paul is not saying that physical or secular things are sinful. Rather, he is saying that any time we separate ourselves from our God-given reason for existence, we fail to live up to our God–given dignity as children of God.

Saint Paul points out that at our Baptism we all received the Holy Spirit by virtue of Jesus' death and resurrection. This allows us to call God, *"Abba,"* as Jesus did when he prayed before he died. If our lives imitate Christ who said, *"not my will, but your will be done"* in the Garden of Gethsemane, then we are living according to the Spirit.

What is the result of living in the Spirit? Saint Paul says it best in Romans 8:11: *"If the Spirit of the one who raised Jesus from the dead dwells in you, the one who raised Christ from the dead will give life to your mortal bodies also, through his Spirit that dwells in you."*

Salesian Concept
The Presence of the Holy Spirit in Our Lives

Saint Francis de Sales taught that, "an interior conversion, a change for the better in one's life, is a true indication of the presence of the Holy Spirit."[19] While we have all received the Holy Spirit at our Baptism, it is up to us to accept the Spirit's guidance in our lives. Preparing for and holding fast to the graces received in the sacraments is a good way to anticipate our future resurrected life.

To that end Saint Francis gives us very important advice on how to prepare to receive the grace of the sacraments in the *Spiritual Conferences:* "The effects of the sacraments are various, although they have but one and the same aim and object which is to unite us to God ...We must know how we ought to prepare properly for the reception of the sacraments. Now the first preparation is purity of intention; the second is attention and the third is humility."[20]

MEDITATION: A SALESIAN METHOD
1. Shift Gears from School Work to Prayer

a. Throw off all your concerns from the school day. *(Relax)*
b. Read Romans 8:7-15

For the concern of the flesh is hostility toward God; it does not submit to the law of God, nor can it; and those who are in the flesh cannot please God. But you are not in the flesh; on the contrary, you are in the spirit, if only the Spirit of God dwells in you. Whoever does not have the Spirit of Christ does not belong to him. But if Christ is in you, although the body is dead because of sin, the spirit is alive because of righteousness. If the Spirit of the one who raised Jesus from the dead dwells in you, the one who raised Christ from the dead will give life to your mortal bodies also, through his Spirit that dwells in you. Consequently, ...we are not debtors to the flesh, to live according to the flesh. For if you live according to the flesh, you will die, but if by the spirit you put to death the deeds of the body, you will live. For those who are led by the Spirit of God are children of God. For you did not receive a spirit of slavery to fall back into fear, but you received a spirit of adoption, through which we cry, "Abba, Father!"

2. Experience Face Time with God

a. Ask for a deeper awareness of God''s presence.
b. Ask for God's inspiration to pray sincerely.

3. Visualize the Story *(Ponder the story's sights, sounds, tastes, smells and feelings.)*

Imagine that you are a Gentile Christian in the Church of Rome after just hearing Paul's letter to the Romans being read for the first time. What does it mean for you practically in terms of your attention that you can only listen to the letter rather than being able to read it? What part of this passage encourages you the most to grow in your faith in Christ?

Later, Paul's words, *"the concern of the flesh is hostility towards God"* grabs your attention. You think of your former life as a non-believer. You recall how you believed solely in the latest trends in philosophy which later always seemed to contradict one another and never offered a final solution to the problem of evil. What problems do you now see in living by the logic of philosophy without the benefits of faith in God? What Christian practices do you now whole-heartedly follow, that you never would have even considered as a pagan philosopher?

You recall a Homeric verse that you used to say frequently. "Eat, drink and be merry, for tomorrow we die." In light of your belief in the resurrection of the body, you now see the sad hopelessness of these words. You also see the failure in Homer's logic. For when, in fact, you did not die, you still had to face the consequences of his poor advice the next day. Sadder still is the fact that you repeated the same mistakes week after week. How has following the guidance of the Holy Spirit freed you from these mistakes? How have the consequences of your actions improved by living according to the righteousness of the Spirit?

You now focus upon the words, *"You did not receive a spirit of slavery to fall back into fear, but you received a spirit of adoption, through which we cry, 'Abba, Father!'"* In light of this, how important is it for you to remain close to Jesus in the Eucharist and the other sacraments of the Church to avoid falling back into your former ways?

4. Express Your Heart *(Write a three sentence spontaneous, heartfelt prayer.)*

What are you feeling as you consider the meaning of calling God *"Abba, Father"* and sharing in the resurrection of Christ? What prayer can you offer to the Holy Spirit for the guidance you will need to faithfully "Live Jesus" according to your identity as a child of God?

5. Be the Change *(Write a resolution that describes what you will do and when.)*

What do you feel you should do in order to live this day well in light of your meditation? Write a concrete resolution that can serve as your response to be open to the Spirit's guidance in making changes for the better in your life.

6. Text a Phrase *(Sum up your meditation into a text of around a 100 characters.)*

State within the confines of this spiritual journal the most helpful insight from your meditation. It can come from the Background, the Salesian Concept or your Salesian Meditation.

7. Create Word Art *(Express your text with visual art, poetry, music, or drama.)*

Express your Text a Phrase in a creative way that will help you recall your meditation with God throughout this day. Your art should help you live faithfully as a Child of God the Father, in order to share in the resurrection of Christ though the power of the Holy Spirit found in the sacraments.

See the color icon for Jesus and Life in the Spirit on page 95.

Visualize the Story *(Write down your insights about God from this meditation.)*

_____

_____

_____

_____

_____

_____

_____

_____

_____

_____

_____

_____

_____

_____

Express Your Heart *(Write a three sentence spontaneous, heartfelt prayer.)*

_____

_____

_____

_____

_____

_____

Be the Change *(Write a resolution that describes what you will do and when.)*

_____

_____

_____

Text a Phrase: *(Sum up your meditation into a text of around a 100 characters.)*

_____

_____

Create Word Art *(Express your text with visual art, poetry, music, or drama.)*

Christ the Alpha and the Omega

Revelation 21:1-4

"I am the Alpha and the Omega." Rev. 22:13

Also the Resurrection and the Life
(John 11:44)

Background

As a Christian do you feel afraid to live as a Christian in front of others? At Mass, do you find it hard to sing audibly? Do you avoid going on youth retreats or joining a youth group? Are you afraid of what others might think of you or what they may say about you behind your back?

John wrote the Book of Revelation to encourage the Christians of his day to accept the risk of their present sufferings for the reward of new life with Christ. The apocalyptic style of John was used in a manner that Christians could understand, but non-Christians could not. Christians, who read Revelation, gained the inspiration they needed to practice their faith in the midst of suffering and ridicule. Thus, the Roman authorities were left dumbfounded by the symbolic visions that revealed how Christ would share his victory over sin and death with the faithful.

The Book of Revelation served the Church well during those times of persecution. Many Christians witnessed to the truth of their faith by willingly giving up their lives in order to inherit new life in the Heavenly Jerusalem. This pattern has been cited often by historians, who have stated, "The blood of the martyrs became the seeds of the Church." The question for us remains: Can we live by the real message of the book of Revelation or will we stand dumbfounded by its hidden symbolism? If we listen to the Church's teachings, preserved for us in Sacred Tradition under the guidance of the Holy Spirit, then we will know the new life faith in Christ brings both in this life and in the resurrection to come.

Salesian Concept
Final Advice about Living the Devout Life

Near the end of the *Introduction to the Devout Life* Saint Francis de Sales uses the example of philosophers who need to declare to the world that they are philosophers, so that people will leave them alone to practice philosophy. De Sales teaches that Christians must make the same kind of declaration if people are going to take them seriously as Christians.

Saint Francis de Sales ends the *Introduction to the Devout Life* by saying, "I beg you, for the love of God, ... By all that is sacred, persevere in your undertaking *(to live a devout Christian life)*. Our days glide away; death and judgment come quickly. Always look upon Heaven, and do not abandon it for the earth. Look into Hell, and do not cast yourself into it for the sake of fleeting things. Look at Jesus Christ, and do not renounce Him for the favors of the world."[21]

MEDITATION: A SALESIAN METHOD
1. Shift Gears from School Work to Prayer

a. Throw off all your concerns from the school day. *(Relax)*
b. Read Revelation 21:1-4 below.

Then I saw a new heaven and a new earth. The former heaven and the former earth had passed away, and the sea was no more. I also saw the holy city, a new Jerusalem, coming down out of heaven from God, prepared as a bride adorned for her husband. I heard a loud voice from the throne saying, "Behold, God's dwelling is with the human race. He will dwell with them and they will be his people and God himself will always be with them (as their God). He will wipe every tear from their eyes, and there shall be no more death or mourning, wailing or pain, (for) the old order has passed away." The one who sat on the throne said, "Behold, I make all things new." Then he said, "Write these words down, for they are trustworthy and true." He said to me, "They are accomplished. I (am) the Alpha and the Omega, the beginning and the end. To the thirsty I will give a gift from the spring of life-giving water. The victor will inherit these gifts, and I shall be his God, and he will be my son."

2. Experience Face Time with God

a. Ask for a deeper awareness of God's presence.
b. Ask for God's inspiration to pray sincerely.

3. Visualize the Story *(Ponder the story's sights, sounds, tastes, smells and feelings.)*

Imagine that you are a Christian in the early Church who has been listening to the book of Revelation being read to you by your church elder*. You are near the end and you can already see that most of the events described in the book have already happened. God the Father, the Lord of History, has already reversed the sentence of the Roman and Jewish authorities by raising Jesus from the dead. Jesus, the Crucified-Risen One, is now exalted and worshipped in heaven. Finally, God is already dwelling with his people, the Church, the Bride of Christ through the Holy Spirit who inspires the churches in joyful worship in spite of persecution. How does all this give you confidence that God, rather than the Roman emperor Diomitian,** is in control and that Jesus, the Alpha and Omega, will have the final say over evil?

* Elders or presbyters performed the role of priests in the early Church.
** Roman Emperor who ruled from CA. A.D. 81-96 and persecuted Christian churches.

You now hear about the *"new heaven and the new earth"* where *"there shall be no more death or mourning, wailing and pain"* because God will *"wipe every tear"* from peoples' eyes by making *"all things new."* How has *"the old order passed away"* after Jesus' resurrection? In what ways do you imagine God consoling you for the things you have suffered in this life?

You reflect further on God's words of death being replaced by life in Christ, especially God's words that *"they* (the above promises) *are already accomplished."* You reflect further on the future meaning of the words, *"The victor will inherit these gifts."* Thus, the victor in this passage cannot be Christ, whose victory over sin and death already happened. The victor must be you, as long as you live by your faith, despite any contrary evidence in the world against God's victory. The only question is: Will you share in God's victory over sin and death? What issues stand between you and ultimate victory? What image from this reading gives you the most encouragement to accept any difficulty or hardship for your faith? What can you do to live like Jesus now in order to share in his victory over sin and death?

4. Express Your Heart *(Write a three sentence spontaneous, heartfelt prayer.)*

What are you feeling as you hear God's promise to wipe every tear from your eyes as child of God? What can you say to God as you pledge to stand by Christ even if it means losing some of the world's favor?

5. Be the Change *(Write a resolution that describes what you will do and when.)*

What do you feel you should do in order to live this day well in light of your meditation? Write one concrete resolution that can serve as your response to place your trust in God's victory despite any fear of rejection and suffering at the hands of an unbelieving world?

6. Text a Phrase *(Sum up your meditation into a text of around a 100 characters.)*

State within the confines of this spiritual journal the most helpful insight from your meditation. It can come from the Background, the Salesian Concept or your Salesian Meditation.

7. Create Word Art *(Express your text with visual art, poetry, music, or drama.)*

Express your Text a Phrase in a creative way that will help you recall your meditation with God throughout this day. Your art should inspire you to overcome any hardship while practicing your faith.

"The Spirit and the bride say, 'Come.'" Rev. 22:17

"I am the Alpha and the Omega." Rev. 22:13

"Behold, I make all things new." Rev. 21:5

See the color icon for Christ the Alpha and Omega on page 95.

Visualize the Story *(Write down your insights about God from this meditation.)*

_____

_____

_____

_____

_____

_____

_____

_____

_____

_____

_____

_____

_____

_____

Express Your Heart *(Write a three sentence spontaneous, heartfelt prayer.)*

_____

_____

_____

_____

_____

_____

Be the Change *(Write a resolution that describes what you will do and when.)*

_____

_____

_____

Text a Phrase: *(Sum up your meditation into a text of around a 100 characters.)*

_____

_____

Create Word Art *(Express your text with visual art, poetry, music, or drama.)*

Introduction to Iconic Lectio by Neil Kane

In the previous pages you have been practicing Lectio Divina or sacred reading of the Word. Now it's time to introduce the practice of Iconic Lectio or sacred reading of an icon or image.

In the Christian Churches of the East, where iconography began, one is said to "write," not paint, a sacred icon. The idea that God communicates or reveals himself through the Word Made Flesh, led to the creation of the icons. Therefore, we can now practice Iconic Lectio by discerning the meaning of an image or icon.

This book takes the sacred iconic tradition from the Byzantine or Eastern Church and alters it slightly to fit our modern times. We read the meaning of a visual logos or image by contemplating it. We experience and seek to understand the significance of colors in the drawing. While beholding the facial expressions of ancient biblical figures like Jesus, Mary or Peter, we can enter more deeply into their experience as well as the mood, the tone and the feeling of the icon.

The goal is to appreciate the icon rather than to intellectually dissect it. Iconic Lectio should use the senses, heart, and the mind. While Lectio Divina uses the imagination to awaken our thoughts and feelings, Iconic Lectio uses our senses to enliven one's mind and heart.

Under each of the pictures you will find two questions to help you enter into the mood, tone and feeling of the icon as well as your own personal awareness of God's activity in your life. Do not feel limited by these questions, as the Holy Spirit may lead you to consider other aspects of the image for your own spiritual welfare. The goal is to come away from your prayerful experience with a new and profound sense of God's presence and love in your life that you can take with you. Therefore, in group discussions you can feel free to share your thoughts as long as you are viewing the same icon everyone else is. Each icon offers many different starting points for meditation. While it is important to keep to some traditional rules of faith, like the Trinity is the Father, Son and Holy Spirit, we do no service by painting God into a confining box based upon one's own past experience.

Finally, you may wish to draw your own icons that serve as a reminder and marker of your spiritual growth. You do not need to be an artist to do this. Just use a combination of basic shapes and biblical phrases that can help you remember your reflections during prayer.

All icons are windows to the sacred.

The Christ Child and Emmanuel
How does the Holy Family reflect hope, peace, joy and love?
How can you prepare to welcome the Christ Child into your heart each Advent?

Jesus, Our Brother and Son of Man
How does this image show Jesus' love for the Father and for us?
What can you do today that could make the Father say, "I am well pleased!"?

89

Christ the Messiah and Son of God Who Calls Us
How is the image of the Cross and the Resurrection seen in this image?
What are the risks and rewards of saying "Yes" to Jesus' invitation to follow Him?

Christ the Teacher and Eschatological or Final Prophet
What do you believe made Jesus such an extraordinary teacher?
Which teachings of Jesus are most meaningful to you?
Which teachings do you find to be the hardest to keep?

Christ the Healer and Lamb of God
How does this icon show that Jesus wants us to be physically and spiritually whole?
How much faith do you have in the Sacrament of Anointing of the Sick to heal?

Christ the Storyteller and the Way and the Truth and the Life
How does this image reflect that God wants us to live out our beliefs in real life?
What is your favorite parable of Jesus?
How does it affect your life as a Christian?

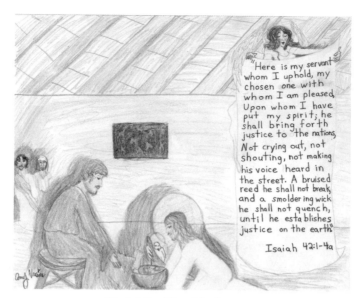

Christ the Humble Servant
How are the goals of your Christian Service Program related to this image?
How can this image help to improve your attitude during your Christian Service?

Christ the Suffering Servant
How does this image reflect that Jesus understands our human sufferings?
How can you ask God for strength to do good in times of trial and suffering?

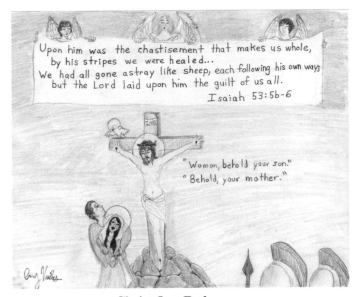

Christ Our Redeemer

How does this image show Jesus' concern for others in the midst of His suffering?
What can you do to better recall Jesus' redeeming love for us all during Mass?

Christ Our Risen Savior

How does this image reflect the joy of Easter and our Resurrection Faith in Christ?
How could your participation at Mass better reflect the joy of the Resurrection?

93

The Risen Christ Who Sends the Holy Spirit
What message do you think Peter is announcing to those gathered at Pentecost?
In what ways do you follow the Holy Spirit's guidance to walk in Christ's path?

Christ in Scripture and Tradition
How do Isaiah's words apply to Christ? To Paul? And to you in particular?
Why do new generations of Christians need to accept the Spirit's guidance to
remain faithful to the Apostolic Tradition it has received about the Risen Christ?

Jesus and Life in the Spirit
How does this icon show the importance of living according to the Spirit?
How can you respond to the Holy Spirit with greater purity, attention and humility?

Christ the Alpha and the Omega
How does this icon reflect humanity's inhumanity as the cause of all suffering?
How does this icon show the Trinity's work to reverse the effects of sin and death?
What tears will God need to wipe from your eyes? For what joys do you long?

95

Appendix Section

The Introduction
to the Devout Life

The Introduction to the Devout Life

Four hundred years ago Saint Francis de Sales wrote the *Introduction to the Devout Life* in response to a religious climate similar to our world today. People were leaving the Church to join the new religions born during the Protestant Reformation. Others turned their attention away from matters of faith to ponder the new discoveries in science and the arts that blossomed during the Renaissance.

This popular move away from Catholicism was not essentially a rejection of the Catholic Faith itself. Rather it was a rejection of the failure of many in the Church to live according to their Catholic faith. The Council of Trent (1545-1563) was called to respond to the issues raised by the Renaissance and Reformation. The result of the Council was not to change what the Catholic Church taught, but rather to change the method used to teach the Catholic Faith in changing times.

The Council of Trent first focused upon the training of priests in seminaries with a uniform catechism. A catechism is a book of theologically true statements about the Catholic Faith organized into questions and grouped by topic. The Catechism had to be developed because during the Middle Ages and up through the Council of Trent, poor education led some priests to mislead the faithful about Church teaching. As a bishop during the Counter-Reformation, Saint Francis de Sales sought to teach the Catholic Faith to both the priests and lay people in a way that was not only faithful to the new catechism, but also responsive to changing times and attitudes.

Francis' popularity as a teacher of spiritual truths led his friends to persuade him to publish a book on the subject of Christian life in the world. The *Introduction to the Devout Life* (1609) was addressed to a fictional woman named Philothea. Philothea means "a soul in love with God." The *Introduction to the Devout Life* is the forerunner of the Vatican II teaching, "the universal call to holiness."[22]

In the *Introduction*, Francis uses imaginative meditations, often focusing upon the affections of one's heart to lead the reader, Philothea or "a soul in love with God" to choose to lead a devout life.

The *Introduction to the Devout Life* covers the following topics:
Part One: The Decision to Live the Devout Life
Part Two: Prayer and Sacraments
Part Three: Choice and Exercise of the Virtues
Part Four: Temptations
Part Five: Self-Renewal

Part I: The Decision to Live the Devout Life

People today often see the Church as being against reason and science, when in truth the Church values both faith and reason as sources of God's revelation. That is why De Sales started the Florimontane Academy where scholars could discuss recent developments in the arts and sciences.[23]

Francis de Sales listening to scholars at the Florimontane Academy.

In the first part of the *Introduction to the Devout Life* Saint Francis de Sales cautions us about accepting false forms of devotion, just as we should be cautious of accepting false representations of what the Catholic Faith teaches and calls us to do.

"Now, little faults one commits at the beginning of an undertaking increase gradually and proportionally as one advances, finally becoming almost irreparable, before all else one must know what the virtue of "true devotion" is. This is especially the case here because, ... there are ... numerous counterfeits of it."[24]

As you most likely already know from this series, De Sales taught that true devotion is simply a true love of God that makes us attentive to do God's will promptly, carefully and often. Saint Francis uses the following analogy to make his point about what true devotion is like: **"Just as a sick man walks only as much as is needed, slowly and painfully, so the sinner, when his sins are forgiven, walks only as much as God commands, ...until devotion is reached. Then, like one in good health, he walks, then runs and jumps about on the way of the Commandments. Finally he goes even further, and moving beyond what is only commanded, he runs along the paths of the counsels and heavenly inspirations."[25]**

Saint Francis warns us that the world only sees Christians avoiding sin, serving others and making sacrifices, but fails to see the love that makes these very actions enjoyable, pleasant and even easy.[26] True devotion, according to De Sales, perfects everything and everyone. If it harms any legitimate task or occupation, it must be a false devotion, since true devotion makes us more peaceful, sincere, faithful and agreeable to our duties in life.[27]

Knowing what true devotion is in reality is one thing, choosing to live a devout life is another. This is why Saint Francis de Sales leads us through a series of ten meditations to rid us of sinful habits and any affection we may have for them. In the final meditation Saint Francis paints a picture of hell without fire and sulfur. Rather De Sales asks us to imagine the people there with faces **"wild with hatred, envy, anger and impurity."** These unfortunate souls despise one another but still **"pay** (the devil) **homage by the various sins they commit."**[28]

On the other hand Saint Francis depicts Jesus in heaven as praying for these poor souls while being surrounded by a vast choir of angels and devout souls from every walk of life. In comparison to those who chose hell, people in Heaven **"live in order, sweetness and joy, loving Our Lord and each other with a holy love."**[29] In the previous meditation, De Sales writes, **"... millions of blessed souls sweetly call you, hoping you will be with them one day... They assure you, that the way to Heaven is not as difficult as the world says."**[30] Imagine your grandparents and loved ones in Heaven gazing on you now. After living a life of devotion, they yearn for you to join them, but worry that any misguided affection for sin will keep you from following their example of faith.

Meditation Ten:
The Choice of a Devout Life

De Sales warns us against our attachments to various sins, **"And thus, poor, weak sinners who abstain from sin for a while ...would really like to be able to commit it without being damned, and they speak about it with pleasure, and consider those who do commit the sin fortunate indeed."**[31] Saint Francis concludes that for such people any future good works will be few and far between with little staying power. Thus, De Sales teaches that to truly rid our souls of sin we must add the power of the Sacrament of Reconciliation to our conversion. A good Confession will help us reject sin and anything associated with it so we can truly resolve to serve God faithfully and **"Live Jesus!"**[32]

Saint Francis concludes **"Just as there is no natural good that can not be corrupted by bad habits, so there is no imperfection... that cannot be overcome..., first of all by God's grace and, cooperating with that, by our own hard work and zeal... May God give you the grace to put this in practice!"**[33]

Part II: Prayer and Sacraments

Step In! follows De Sales' view of mental prayer.

Saint Francis de Sales immediately states, **"Prayer places our intelligence in the divine light and exposes our will to the warmth of divine love. It is the best way to purge our intelligence of its ignorance and our will of its bad affections."**[34] Again, De Sales points to the importance of reason, but in true Salesian fashion, reminds us that our reason needs to be balanced by faith and love in God.

Saint Francis taught that our prayer life should reflect this same balance between faith and reason by urging us to practice mental prayer that touches both the mind and heart rather than just saying memorized prayers. He especially recommended meditation upon the life, passion, death and resurrection of Jesus each morning when we would be more refreshed and less distracted by our daily tasks.

The first step in prayer is always to make ourselves aware of God's presence with us. One way is to simply state with love, **"God is truly here and I am preparing myself to speak to him and listen to him."**[35] Another way is to always remember that God is truly present wherever we are as Saint Paul says in Acts 17:28, **"For in Him (God) we live, move and exists."** De Sales also suggests thinking of the Risen Jesus gazing upon us as we pray or using our imaginations by picturing Jesus sitting next to us in the same way we imagine our friends being close to us when they are absent.[36]

"In our remaining close to our Lord by meditation, listening to His words, contemplating His actions and His affections, we will learn, with His grace, to speak, to act and to will like Him."[37] As a college student at the University of Padua, Francis de Sales made use of mental prayer to excel in school and to maintain good relationships with all. He called it the Preparation of the Day. He began each morning by thanking God for giving him a new day and planned to live it as a preparation to spend eternity with God. He would seek any possibility of serving God while remaining faithful to his duties and responsibilities. He would also try to foresee any dangers of offending God in his day through sin. Finally, he would make a concrete plan to put his prayerful thoughts into action.[38]

You can see that for Saint Francis de Sales it is not enough to have good thoughts and feelings during our prayers. Rather it is essential that we act upon our prayerful thoughts by making resolutions to help others. De Sales writes, **"If I am resolved, for example, to be gentle in order to win over the heart of someone who has offended me, I shall try, on this very day, to encounter him and so as to greet him pleasantly, and if that is not possible, I shall at least say something good about him and pray to God on his behalf."**[39]

Saint Francis de Sales went even further by telling us to do everything in our power to avoid an empty and fruitless prayer life. De Sales urges us to make an Examination of Conscience later in the day, but definitely before going to bed. In true Salesian Optimism, De Sales does not use this exercise merely to point out our faults. Rather he urges us to begin on a positive note, thanking God for any good done during that day. Only then are we to recall any wrongdoing or sin in thought, word or deed. The point is to make us accountable to do the good we planned during our morning prayer rather than to make us feel guilty.[40]

Saint Francis ends Part Two of the *Introduction to the Devout Life* teaching about the Sacrament of the Eucharist and the Sacrament of Reconciliation. De Sales calls the Mass **"the sun of all spiritual exercises,"**[41] and states, **"Prayer made in union with this divine sacrifice has incalculable power."**[42] Another helpful piece of advice Saint Francis gives concerning the Eucharist is that, **"If you cannot go in person, unite yourself to the intentions of all Christians and make the same acts of devotion you would make** (like meditating on Bible readings for Mass) **as if you were there."**[43] Ultimately, De Sales urges us to receive Communion frequently: **"The Christians who will be damned will be without excuse when the just Judge makes them realize the mistake they made in dying spiritually, since it was so easy for them to remain spiritually alive and healthy by eating his Body, left to them for this very purpose!"**[44]

Saint Francis speaks similarly about the Sacrament of Reconciliation, **"Never permit your heart to be affected by sin for long since you have such an easy remedy within reach."**[45]

Praying the Rosary attentively can help us meditate on the life of Christ and learn to speak, act and will like Jesus.

Part III: Choice and Exercise of the Virtues

The section on virtue is by far the longest part of the *Introduction to the Devout Life*. With over forty chapters to cover in two short pages, let us focus only on relevant issues for young people today.

De Salcs begins by stating that "**Charity** (true love of God) **never enters a heart without bringing with it all the others virtues, empowering them and marshalling them as needed ... When charity waters one's soul, it produces virtuous works, but each in its** (proper) **season.**"[46] Saint Francis teaches the following about virtues:

As a Doctor of the Church Saint Francis' writings are free from any moral, spiritual or doctrinal errors.

- While most virtues should be limited to certain situations, the **"little virtues of gentleness, temperance, honesty and humility are the sort that should characterize all our actions."**[47]
- We must practice virtue in a way that fits the duties in our life.
- We should choose the most excellent virtues not the most showy.
- It is not enough to practice the virtues in visible, exterior actions. Our practice of the virtues must also be reflected in our interior dispositions or attitudes.
- When tempted by a particular sin, we should practice the opposite virtue, pray sincerely and attend the sacraments lovingly.[48]
- We must practice virtues faithfully but also prudently by using the guides God has given us like the Church or a spiritual director. [49]

In terms of individual virtues, Saint Francis writes positively and practically about the Salesian virtues of humility before God and gentleness towards our neighbors. **"Nothing can humble us so much before God's mercy as His countless blessings."**[50] Rather than puffing us up with pride, the knowledge of God's mercy and love makes us grateful and willing to imitate Jesus' gentle and humble heart. De Sales warns us that some people **"think that they are humble and gentle when they are really not so. This can be seen to be the case when, in spite of their appearance of gentleness and humility, they become irritated and annoyed at the slightest contradictory word or the least offense."**[51]

De Sales gives us an even more difficult teaching for those who want to excel in virtue and devotion called loving one's abjection. To be truly humble and gentle means that we need not only to act in humble and gentle ways, but that we also must accept the consequences that these virtues bring. This completes the Salesian concept linked to our meditation on the Rich Man and Lazarus. It is not enough to welcome the poor into our homes; we must also accept any ridicule that comes as a result of this act from others, even our friends. Saint Francis gives another timely example of real love of abjection: **"In a group of young people, those who do not participate in the general dissoluteness** (immorality) **are roundly mocked."**[52] De Sales would have us consider how good it would be to accept this difficult practice today in terms of underage drinking or pre-marital sex.

Chastity is another virtue that is often misunderstood and ridiculed today. Saint Francis wrote passionately about the goodness of both human love and sexuality as a reflection of God's divine goodness and love. Therefore, he can help us to view chastity as more than just the practice of avoiding sex before marriage to seeing chastity as the interior virtue that helps us be who we are and be that well. De Sales writes the following about chastity: **"Nothing is so beautiful as purity, and purity in human beings is chastity. It is called integrity, while its opposite is called corruption."**[53]

In order to avoid this corruption, we need to avoid reckless curiosity and train our hearts to reject impure pleasures by reminding ourselves that chastity is better than anything opposed to it. One just has to look at the Tiger Woods scandal to see the truth behind this. If we truly seek lives of chastity, we need to **"seek the company of chaste and virtuous persons, and to meditate often on the word of God."**[54] You will fulfill the second task by completing the meditations in this book. The first task is entirely up to you.

This brings us to the topic of friendship, De Sales thought enough about it in terms of Christian life that he devoted six chapters to it. Saint Francis tells us **"for those who live in the midst of the world and yet strive for true virtue, it is necessary to ally themselves to one another by a holy and sacred friendship through which they stimulate, assist, and encourage each other toward good."**[55] While De Sales maintained good relationships with all, he developed certain "spiritual friendships" with Saint Jane de Chantal, Saint Vincent de Paul and others. As Salesians we should do the same.

Part IV: Temptations

As a spiritual director Saint Francis de Sales counseled many people who wanted to turn away from sin and embrace a life of holiness and devotion. After learning about the first three parts of the *Introduction to the Devout Life,* perhaps you realize it is time to live a more faithful life as a Christian. However, as soon as we decide to live virtuous lives, De Sales warns us that we will surely face temptations against that decision, and some of these will come from people claiming to be our friends.

Developing and maintaining spiritual friendships is a strong defense against temptation.

"**As soon as the world perceives that you desire to pursue the road to holiness, it will fire a thousand darts at you … you are going to sink into sadness, you will lose all prestige, … you will grow old before your time and your affairs will suffer for it … They will add that you must live like the rest of the world … and that you can be saved without so many practices.**"[56]

Saint Francis de Sales teaches that in order to stand up to these temptations, we need to have firm courage. De Sales tells us that if we persevere in the face of these temptations we will "**find true joy before long and will recognize that a single day spent in God's love is worth more than a thousand years of this world's life.**"[57]

In order to overcome temptations Saint Francis points out the steps that lead us to sin, namely: 1) the temptation itself, 2) any pleasure we experience as part of the temptation and 3) the consent we give to it. De Sales warns us against confusing temptations with sins, since this can lead us to discouragement. Thus when it comes to temptation he says: "**Even should temptation last all our life, it does not make us disagreeable to God, provided it does not please us and we do not consent to it. Why? Because in temptation we do not act; we are acted upon. If we do not take pleasure in it, we commit no fault.**"[58]

Saint Francis de Sales also gives really helpful advice for people who have given into temptations often or those who are experiencing great temptations. In his practical and optimistic manner he writes,

"Have you ever seen a great **brazier** (of coal or wood) **covered with ashes? When you go to it to look for fire, you have trouble finding the least spark; nevertheless, it often contains enough to revive the embers.** It is the same with charity, our spiritual life, in the midst of great temptations. These great temptations, which may provoke pleasure in the inferior part of the soul** (our senses and emotions), **seem to cover everything with ashes and to reduce God's love to almost nothing."**[59] Yet De Sales says, our inclination to love God above all things, while appearing to be nowhere, continues to dwell **"in the center of the heart, and in the interior part of the soul."**[60]

The easiest remedy for fighting temptations according to Saint Francis de Sales is to simply remove yourself from the temptation without arguing with its source. De Sales suggests keeping ourselves busy with our daily tasks and later speaking about the nature and source of these temptations with our confessor or a spiritual director. If the temptation persists, we must continue to say no to it. Saint Francis writes, **"Just as a young woman cannot be married as long as she says no, the soul, even when troubled, cannot be overcome as long as it says no! ... So too, the soul which is assailed by temptation does not amuse itself by responding to and debating with the tempter. It simply turns toward Jesus Christ, her Spouse, repeating her fidelity and desire to be solely His forever."**[61]

If we truly want to defeat our greatest temptations, De Sales advises us to focus first on resisting smaller and more frequent temptations. Saint Francis writes, **"It is easier to avoid bearing false witness before the courts than to avoid lying in conversations ... It is easier to avoid outright slander than to avoid despising our neighbor a bit."**[62] To overcome smaller temptations De Sales tells us to keep our focus on doing God's will in the present moment.

When small temptations appear suddenly, Saint Francis urges us to practice the opposite virtue. Nowhere is this more important than when we are tempted by anxiety, of which De Sales wrote, **"After sin, this is the greatest evil that can befall us."**[63] At these times we should patiently place **"our confidence more in God's Providence than in our own industry, care and efforts."**[64] If our anxiety comes from not finding joy in spiritual exercises, Saint Francis tells us, **"Where there is less joy in our actions, there is, nevertheless, undoubtedly more virtue, and thus greater merit."**[65] Saint Francis would also urge us to renew ourselves through wholesome recreation.

Part V: Self-Renewal

As we end our summary of the *Introduction to the Devout Life,* it would be good to take into account which teachings of Saint Francis de Sales were the most meaningful and helpful for you. As you think about these Salesian teachings, you may already realize that without constant care and attention, you can fall back into your old habits. In view of this, De Sales compares our spiritual life to clocks in his time. No matter how excellent, they still needed rewinding twice a day as well as yearly maintenance to run at their peak.

Saint Francis de Sales urges us to renew our resolution to love God every year with the help of a confessor or spiritual director.

"It is important, at least once a year, to examine in depth one's dispositions so as to correct dispositions which might have slipped in, and to enable the oil of grace to penetrate there with the Sacraments of Reconciliation and Holy Eucharist. This exercise will renew your strength weakened by time, reanimate your heart, cause renewed growth in your good resolutions and enable your virtues to flourish."[66]

Saint Francis reminds us that just as the souls in the Heavenly Jerusalem rejoiced in our first resolution to serve God, how much more they will rejoice in hearing us renew this promise each and every year. De Sales also asks us to look back on the results of our decision to live the devout life: **"Is it not happiness to speak to God in prayer, to have a desire to love Him, to have mastered your passions, to have avoided many sins and troubles of conscience and to have received Holy Communion so much more frequently?"**[67]

Next Saint Francis leads us to consider our behavior and the state of our heart towards God, ourselves and our neighbor. In doing this we are to ask for the help of the Holy Spirit to advance in self-knowledge and to grow in holiness, even if just a little at a time. De Sales suggests that we take our time examining these things and even keep a journal about what we discover. This will help us recall issues more accurately so we can get more helpful advice on making good resolutions.[68]

In addition Saint Francis wants us to consider the following before renewing our protestation and resolution to love and serve God:

1) The excellence of the soul, **"which is made for God. What a misfortune for it to be satisfied with less than God!"**[69]

2) The excellence of virtue, which alone can give us lasting happiness in this world because patience is more noble than vengeance and generosity is sweeter than greed.[70]

3) The example of the saints, our models of holiness, who were once as new to the devout life as we are now. Why should we not follow their example in keeping faithful to our resolution to serve God?[71]

4) The love of Jesus Christ that led Him to suffer for us all as well as the necessary graces given to us by God the Father that not only makes our spiritual life possible but also fruitful as well.[72]

5) The eternal love of God for you in particular which Saint Francis writes, **"God has loved you with an eternal love; even before His Son suffered and died for you on the Cross, He loved you infinitely... Your resolutions are, therefore, the fruit of God's eternal design for you. How dear they ought to be to you!"**[73]

6) De Sales ends these considerations by telling us to simply renew our resolution to serve God in the presence of Our Lady, our guardian angel and the saints after making a general confession of our sins and uniting our hearts to Jesus in the Sacrament of the Eucharist. Saint Francis explains the power of our resolutions to serve God by saying, **"If we keep them, they will keep us; if they live in our heart, our heart will live."**[74]

In the last chapter of the *Introduction to the Devout Life*, Saint Francis de Sales provides practical advice on living a life of devotion. Just as philosophers openly declare themselves to be philosophers so they can live as they wish, Christians must openly declare themselves to be Christians, so people will allow them to live as Christians. If people say that we do not need so many spiritual exercises to be saved, Saint Francis states that we should not deny this truth. Rather he says that we should simply state that we need these exercises due to our own spiritual weaknesses that require more support than others need.[75]

Finally, De Sales reminds us, **"When the road to holiness seems difficult to you, repeat after Saint Francis of Assisi: 'All the troubles and all the sufferings of this earth are as nothing compared to the blessings to come.' Live Jesus, with the Father and the Holy Spirit!"**[76]

Application for Today Questions:

Part I: The Decision to Live the Devout Life

1. Name some aspects of faith that Catholics have difficulty doing promptly, carefully and often.
2. What would your grandparents and great-grandparents in heaven say t you now about the importance of worshipping God sincerely at Mass?
3. Why is it so important to remove our affection for sin through Confession?
4. How can the practice of true devotion perfect us in our duties at home in our work at school and in all our relationships?

Part II: Prayer and Sacraments

1. How can meditating on your favorite Gospel story enlighten your mind about God's love for you and rid your heart of its affection for sin?
2. Which Salesian method of recalling God's presence works best for you?
3. How do the Preparation of the Day and Examination of Conscience relate in a similar way to the Sacraments of Eucharist and Reconciliation?

Part III: Choice and Exercise of the Virtues

1. Which Salesian teaching on virtue makes the most sense to you?
2. What can we learn from the example of Jesus about being truly humble in the story of Jesus washing his disciples' feet?
3. What can we learn from the example of Jesus about being truly gentle in the story of Jesus' Agony in the Garden?
4. How encouraging are your friends in helping you live a virtuous and moral life in terms of avoiding underage drinking and/or premarital sex?

Part IV: Temptations

1. How can the spiritual activities that draw us closest to God give us the courage to practice our faith in the face of temptations and ridicule?
2. Which is the most helpful piece of Salesian advice concerning temptation?
3. Which is the most encouraging piece of advice from Saint Francis de Sales concerning temptation and sin?

Part V: Self-Renewal

1. What is the wisdom in Saint Francis de Sales' advice to renew our desire to live a devout life daily, weekly, monthly and yearly?
2. How would living in a devout Christian manner improve your life?
3. What is your action plan for facing any spiritual difficulties that occur?

While coloring this icon of Jesus use your imagination to see God's presence during your busy school day.

Dwell upon good thoughts of God's love for you. Enjoy this moment free from your normal school work.

Write a brief prayer in response to the state of your heart at the present moment.

Write a resolution to practice virtue more promptly, carefully and often in your daily tasks.

Try your own word art using basic shapes and words for Matt 11:29.

Bibliography

Catholic Controversy, St. Francis de Sales' Defense of the Faith. Translated by Henry Benedict Mackey, Rockford, Ill.: TAN Books and Publishers, 1989.

Introduction to the Devout Life. Tr. Fr. Joseph D. Bowler, OSFS and Fr. Lewis S. Fiorelli, OSFS. Rockford, IL: TAN Books and Publishers, 1990.

Letters of Spiritual Direction. Tr. Peronne Marie Thibert, VHM*.* New York: Paulist Press, 1988.

New American Bible. Ed. Rev. Louis Hartmann, C.SS.R., Washington, DC: World Bible Publishers, Inc.,1987.

Pope *Benedict XVI. 40th anniversary of Dei Verbum. www.vatican.va/phome_en.htm., 1993.*

St. Francis de Sales: A Testimony by St Chantal. Tr. Elizabeth Stopp. Hyattsville, MD: Institute of Salesian Studies, 1967.

Saltarelli, Bishop Michael. *Celebrating the Year of Saint Paul June 28, 2008-June 29, 2009. Catholic Diocese of Wilmington, January 2008.*

Select Salesian Subjects: Over 800 Passages by or about Francis de Sales and Jane de Chantal Selected from Fifty Sources. Compiled by Sr. Mary Grace Flynn, VHM. Stella Niagara, NY: DeSales Resources and Ministries, 2007.

Selected Letters. Tr. Elizabeth Stopp. New York: Harper and Brothers, 1960.

Sermons of St. Francis de Sales for Advent and Christmas. Edited by Lewis S. Fiorelli, translated by the Nuns of the Visitation [Frances Therese Leary], with a preface by Robert E. Mulvee. Sermons of St. Francis de Sales, vol. 4. Rockford, Ill.: Tan Books, 1987.

Spiritual Conferences of Saint Francis de Sales. Translation by Father William J. Ruhl, OSFS from the French text reconstructed by Roger Devos. Washington D.C.: De Sales School of Theology, 1997.

Spiritual Directory. Tr. Rev. John P. Connolly, OSFS. Wilmington, DE: Wilmington-Philadelphia Province of the Oblates of Saint Francis de Sales, 1974.

Special Personal Acknowledgements

Meditation format adapted from Salesian Prayers of the Heart
by Father Michael Murray, OSFS De Sales Spirituality Center

Salesian themed stained glass images on pages 96, 98, 101, 102, 104 and 106 from the Visitation Monastery in Annecy, France, courtesy of Father Robert McGilvary, OSFS

Stained glass images of the Sacred Heart of Jesus on page 99 from Saints Simon and Jude Parish in West Chester, PA and Saint Francis de Sales "Live Jesus, Whom I Love" on page 100 from the Oblate Chapel in Childs, MD taken by Tom Vresics

Iconic Lectio Description on page 88 by Neil Kane

Icon of Jesus on page 109 by Amy Vresics

Proofread by Mary Ann Sianni and Betsy Diemer

Publication Advisors: Betsy Diemer, Ed Gordon, Susan Gardner,
Father J. Christian Beretta, OSFS and Father Michael Donavan, OSFS

Production Advisors: Herb Andersesn and Mary Facciolo

IT Advisors Brother Harry Schneider, OSFS, Chris Brower and Mike Mason

Translators the icon on pages 68 and 94: Neil Kane (Latin), Patrick Kennedy, OSFS (Greek and Hebrew) Attica and Stephen Menicucci (Arabic) and Tedesse Mulat (Ethiopian Amharic Script)

God Be Praised!

110

Notes

1. *Sermons of Saint Francis de Sales for Christmas and Advent,* Christmas Eve Sermon 1620.
2. *Introduction to the Devout Life,* Part Four, Chapter 9.
3. Dogmatic Constitution on the Church, Lumen Gentium, Chapter 5.
4. This is one of those oft quoted sayings of De Sales for which it is difficult to find a specific citation. The closest I can find is See also Letter of October 13, 1604, Elisabeth Stopp, *Selected Letters* (New York: Harper and Harper, 1960), p. 61: "We must love all that God loves, and He loves our vocation; so let us love it too and not waste our energy hankering after a different sort of life, but get on with our own job."
5. *Introduction to the Devout Life,* Part Three, Chapter 1.
6. *Saint Francis de Sales: A Testimony* by Saint Chantal, page 70.
7. *Introduction to the Devout Life,* Part Three, Chapter 15.
8. *Saint Francis de Sales: A Testimony* by Saint Chantal, page 69.
9. *Introduction to the Devout Life,* Part Three, Chapter 2.
10. *Introduction to the Devout Life,* Part One, Chapter 13.
11. *Selected Letters*, page 52.
12. *Catholic Controversy,* Part One, Chapter 6, Section 1.
13. *Introduction to the Devout Life*, Part Two, Chapter 14.
14. *Introduction to the Devout Life*, Part Two, Chapter 14.
15. *Introduction to the Devout Life*, Part Two, Chapter 21.
16. *Introduction to the Devout Life*, Part Two, Chapter 21.
17. *Introduction to the Devout Life,* Part Two, Chapter 13 and Part Three, Chapter 26.
18. *Catholic Controversy,* Part Three, Chapter 1, Section 1.
19. Sermons 47; X.O., p.72
20. *Spiritual Conferences,* Conference Eighteen.
21. *Introduction to the Devout Life,* Part V, Chapter 18.
22. *Praying with Francis de Sales,* pages 13-27.
23. *Praying with Francis de Sales,* page 18.
24. *Introduction to the Devout Life,* Part One, Chapter 1.
25. *Introduction to the Devout Life,* Part One, Chapter 1.
26. *Introduction to the Devout Life,* Part One, Chapter 2.
27. *Introduction to the Devout Life,* Part One, Chapter 3.
28. *Introduction to the Devout Life,* Part One, Chapter 18.
29. *Introduction to the Devout Life,* Part One, Chapter 18.
30. *Introduction to the Devout Life,* Part One, Chapter 17.
31. *Introduction to the Devout Life,* Part One, Chapter 7.
32. *Introduction to the Devout Life,* Part One, Chapter 20.
33. *Introduction to the Devout Life,* Part One, Chapter 24.
34. *Introduction to the Devout Life,* Part Two, Chapter 1.
35. *Introduction to the Devout Life,* Part Two, Chapter 2.
36. *Introduction to the Devout Life,* Part Two, Chapter 2.
37. *Introduction to the Devout Life,* Part Two, Chapter 1.
38. *Introduction to the Devout Life,* Part Two, Chapter 10.
39. *Introduction to the Devout Life,* Part Two, Chapter 8.
40. *Introduction to the Devout Life,* Part Two, Chapter 11.
41. *Introduction to the Devout Life,* Part Two, Chapter 14.
42. *Introduction to the Devout Life,* Part Two, Chapter 14.
43. *Introduction to the Devout Life,* Part Two, Chapter 14.
44. *Introduction to the Devout Life,* Part Two, Chapter 20.
45. *Introduction to the Devout Life,* Part Two, Chapter 19.

Notes

46. *Introduction to the Devout Life*, Part Three, Chapter 1.
47. *Introduction to the Devout Life*, Part Three, Chapter 1.
48. *Introduction to the Devout Life*, Part Three, Chapter 1.
49. *Introduction to the Devout Life*, Part Three, Chapter 12.
49. *Introduction to the Devout Life*, Part Three, Chapter 5.
50. *Introduction to the Devout Life*, Part Three, Chapter 8.
51. *Introduction to the Devout Life*, Part Three, Chapter 6.
52. *Introduction to the Devout Life*, Part Three, Chapter 12.
53. *Introduction to the Devout Life*, Part Three, Chapter 13.
54. *Introduction to the Devout Life*, Part Three, Chapter 19.
55. *Introduction to the Devout Life*, Part Four, Chapter 1.
56. *Introduction to the Devout Life*, Part Four, Chapter 2.
57. *Introduction to the Devout Life*, Part Four, Chapter 3.
58. *Introduction to the Devout Life*, Part Four, Chapter 3.
59. *Introduction to the Devout Life*, Part Four, Chapter 3.
60. *Introduction to the Devout Life*, Part Four, Chapter 7.
61. *Introduction to the Devout Life*, Part Four, Chapter 8.
62. *Introduction to the Devout Life*, Part Four, Chapter 11
63. *Introduction to the Devout Life*, Part Four, Chapter 11.
64. *Introduction to the Devout Life*, Part Four, Chapter 18.
65. *Introduction to the Devout Life*, Part Five, Chapter 1.
66. *Introduction to the Devout Life*, Part Five, Chapter 2.
67. *Introduction to the Devout Life*, Part Five, Chapter 3.
68. *Introduction to the Devout Life*, Part Five, Chapter 10.
69. *Introduction to the Devout Life*, Part Five, Chapter 3.
70. *Introduction to the Devout Life*, Part Five, Chapter 11.
71. *Introduction to the Devout Life*, Part Five, Chapter 13.
72. *Introduction to the Devout Life*, Part Five, Chapter 14.
73. *Introduction to the Devout Life*, Part Five, Chapter 15.
74. *Introduction to the Devout Life*, Part Five, Chapter 18.
75. *Introduction to the Devout Life*, Part Five, Chapter 18.